CHRISTIANA AWDRY'S H...

CHRISTIANA AWDRY'S HOUSEHOLD BOOK

Edited and annotated by
Margaret Jensen

Illustrations by Jeanette Litterick

EX LIBRIS PRESS

Published in 1995
by Ex Libris Press
1 The Shambles
Bradford on Avon
Wiltshire

Design and Typesetting by Ex Libris Press

Cover printed by Shires Press, Trowbridge, Wiltshire.

Printed and bound in Britain by
Cromwell Press, Broughton Gifford, Wiltshire.

ISBN 0 948578 70 X

FOR ISOBEL – until we merrily meet – and for HANS

Contents

Sweet & Savoury Preserves

Contents

Drinks

Contents

Cosmetics & Domestics

Cures & Remedies

Introduction

On 20 September 1721 Ambrose Awdry, gentleman, was made a
freeman of the Borough of Chippenham and 'the said Ambrose
Awdry not being borne within this borough, nor married with a
widow or daughter of a recorded inhabitant of this borough, nor
served as an apprentice for the space of seven years' he was required to pay 'for recording and registering his name £1:00:00'.
Ambrose, whose father John Awdry was described as a 'mercer',
came from Melksham and was a great-great-grandson of John
Awdry who was Vicar of Melksham in the early part of the
seventeenth century. In 1723 Ambrose Awdry was elected Bailiff
of the Borough of Chippenham and the records show that in 1728
'Ambrose Awdry one of ye Burgesses of this Borough departed this
life': he was just thirty-six years old.

On 22 July 1721, just two months before Ambrose Awdry
became a freeman of Chippenham, the *London Journal* was
publishing 'An Excellent Medicine against the Plague', an item
interesting and important enough for some other member of the
Awdry family to keep and record in a book of remedies, cures,
household hints and recipes that has survived to the present day.
Recipes for everything from Apricock Cakes and Apopletick Water
to Wafers, Wiggs and Pickled Walnuts were written in minute
detail in a large leather-covered book of over three hundred pages.
Though there is an index there is very little attempt to separate
the four hundred and seventy recipes and remedies into different
categories. The book begins with a few recipes followed by some
thirty pages of remedies but even here a recipe for 'Fish Sauce' can
be found between the instructions for cleaning blond lace and for
dying gloves purple. In later pages 'A Bisket Cake' is followed by
'A Cure for Jaundice', and the instructions for making 'Liquid
Soap' share a page with 'Oyster Sausages' and 'Calves Head like
Brawn'.

There are four different styles of hand-writing, from a spidery eighteenth century hand used for the first half of the book and the index to a more elegant [and possibly later] copper-plate but there is nothing to show the identities of those writers. The only date mentioned, apart from 22 July, 1721, is in the instructions for making 'Asmatick Pills' by which Mrs Cook was cured in 1743 by Dr Boerhave who 'was reckoned the best of his time and lived in Utrick [Utrecht] in Holland'. Other clues to the manuscript's date can be found in the style and pattern of the book's engraved binding which is identical to others which can be firmly placed in the middle years of the eighteenth century. The recipes and remedies range from some which are near medieval in character to others whose counterparts can be found in the standard eighteenth century cookery books such as those by Hannah Glasse, Elizabeth Raffald or Patrick Lambe.

Many of these recipes and cures were obtained on personal recommendation: Lady Westmorland's Strengthening Plaster for the Back of 'breeding women', a cure for Ague and Fever obtained from Sir Robert Cotton of Cheshire, 'a very good and charitable man', Lady Frederick's Receipt for the Bite of a Mad Dog and Mr Lathom's Poultice for Man or Beast. There is the remedy by which Miss Lisle, 'sister to the Commodore' was cured of 'loss of limbs by cold' and Miss Bathurst contributes the cure for a 'weak decaying constitution' which helped a young lady who had 'been carried to and from bed for four months'. A further four doctors are mentioned: we have Doctor Ratcliffe's 'Bitter for a Bad Digestion', Doctor Cheney's Burgundy for 'Stomatick Gout', Doctor Lowers' 'Tincture for the Cholick' and from Doctor Mead a 'Very Good Drink for a Consumption' as well as a 'Receipt for the Bite of a Mad Dog'. For those who preferred 'An Infallible Cure' for the same problem there are very detailed instructions from the Reverend W.Post 'of Great Chervell' and 'The Pomade Divine' which is almost the last remedy in the book was, apparently, used by Mrs Delmé to great effect: she 'cured a person going to be cut for a fistula by it and a Man who was near starved by a sore mouth of five or six months standing'.

*   *   *

In trying to trace these shadowy eighteenth century characters I have had limited success. The Awdry family was an extensive one: the Ambrose Awdry of Chippenham who died in 1728 was one of six children. His father John Awdry was the eldest of ten. A younger brother of John, also named Ambrose was born in 1664 and, by his marriage to Mary Selfe, had five children. The eldest child, a son, was also baptised Ambrose. That Ambrose's second child, a son born in 1726 was – almost inevitably – named Ambrose. When the youngest Ambrose died three years later the name was used for his younger brother, born in 1729. In 1761 that Ambrose Awdry married Christiana, daughter of Peter Delmé of Erlestoke. For those interested in naming traditions the names Ambrose, Peter and Delmé continued as baptismal names in the Awdry family through the next three generations. Ambrose and Christiana's tenth child, William Henry, born in 1778 was the great-great-grandfather of the manuscript's present owner. It seems possible that Christiana Awdry [née Delmé] was the original owner of the manuscript. Certainly some of the recipes and remedies were obtained from people who lived close to that branch of the family or who were connected with them in some other way.

A link between the Awdry family and the Earl of Westmoreland can be found in the ownership of land and titles in Seend. In the sixteenth century the Manors of Seend and Seend Row were owned by Sir Henry Sharington of Lacock Abbey: in 1599 he gave them to his grandaughter Mary Mildmay on her marriage to Sir Francis Fane, Earl of Westmorland. In the years after the Civil War Sir Francis Fane's son, Mildmay, Earl of Westmorland sold the family lands in Seend, possibly to help pay the fines levied on him for his support of the Royalist cause. The Manor of Seend Row was purchased by the Awdry family and, in 1761, given to Ambrose Awdry on his marriage to Christiana Delmé, who appears to have obtained the Countess of Westmorland's house as well as her 'Strengthening Plaster for the Back of Breeding Women'.

The Reverend W. Post, source of one of the cures for the bite of a mad dog, was easier to trace: the parish registers of Great Cheverill record in 1733 the birth of a son, Walter, and the following year a daughter, Jemimah, to Anna Dorothea, wife of the Reverend Walter Post. In 1756 Jemimah Post married John

Shergold, gentleman, of Little Cheverill. The Reverend Post was three times forced to seek warrants from the magistrates: in 1745 he had been robbed of 'board and other things'. Three years later on January 30 1748 he sought a warrant against Margaret Mattock 'touching in particular the said Margaret Mattock's stealing turnips out of his enclosed ground'. She was 'convicted but forgiven by the complainant' – and only two weeks later repeated the offence! This time when 'convicted for stealing of turnips ... the property of the said Reverend Mr Post' she was 'ordered to be whipped publicly not exceeding ten lashes' but again the generous Reverend Mr Post forgave her. Some years later he was to have a disturbing experience which he recorded in his own words:

> On Thursday October 23 1766 about ten o'clock in the evening my neighbour in the house inhabited by the late Mr James Bartlett sent his new-born son to my house by his nurse to be privately baptized, insisting I should make him a Christian immediately as the child was ill [he said] and the nurse confirmed the same. The boy was named George but my neighbour would not let me know his own Christian and sur-name, nor the name of the Babe's mother tho' I requested it once and again by message in order to be enabled [I informed him] to register the Baptism. I'm told my neighbour has once or twice only [since he has been in my parish about six months] declar'd his name to be William Woddeston or Wooddesson or Woodson and his servant by whom he had the child went by the name of Jane or Jinny but of her surname I never could learn anything. As I thought myself obliged to register the child in my Church book, I thought it not improper to account for my manner of Entrance there.

The Reverend Mr Post remained in Great Cheverill until his death in 1772 at the age of seventy-eight. His memorial tablet in the church there is both sad and puzzling since it records the death of the Reverend Mr Post's first wife, Anna Dorothea, on 14 May 1744 at the age of thirty-two and his second wife, Elizabeth, on 11 December 1761, at the age of one hundred and twelve! The local explanation is that this is the result of the stone-mason's careless transcription of forty-two – unless of course the widowed clergyman really did choose a second wife some forty-five years older than himself. The memorial tablet also records the untimely deaths of the Reverend Mr Post's daughter, Jemimah at the age of thirty-six, and four grand-daughters, none of whom lived to be older than seven years.

Though I have unravelled some mysteries others remain: in researching ingredients one or two of the medical ingredients proved impossible to trace and I was unable to find definitions of 'pumeroy' and 'paplin'. The range and variety of ingredients is surprising though there are notable omissions. While there are recipes using truffles, pomegranates and pistachio nuts not one uses potatoes. There is no mention of tomatoes although they had been grown in this country since the sixteenth century. Sir Richard Weston in 1778 lists them as 'love-apples' under the heading 'Annual Flowers' and just a few years later Jane Austen was including enthusiastic comments about 'tomatas' in a letter to her sister, Cassandra.

Vegetables generally are under-represented: on the other hand there are numerous recipes using apricots, peaches, quinces, apples, pears, gooseberries, red and white currants, strawberries, raspberries, oranges, lemons, cherries, barberries, elderberries, plums, figs and damsons. Sweet preserves and sweet dishes – cakes, biscuits and puddings of various kinds – outnumber the savoury. In transcription I have retained the wording of the original with very little alteration but have modernised the spelling and punctuation for the sake of clarity. Thus 'cian pepper' has become 'cayenne', 'musharoons' are 'mushrooms' and 'sparemint' has become 'spearmint'. The spelling of spearmint offers an insight into eighteenth century pronunciation as does the rhyming of 'observe' and 'starve' in the cure 'for an Asthma'.

In using the manuscript as the basis for this book I have attempted to create a context, some idea of the world in which the collection was compiled. The 'voice' of contemporary letters, newspaper reports or journals provides a background for the 'voices' of the manuscript. It is perhaps in the cures and remedies that these voices emerge most clearly: the 'Infallible Cure for the Bite of a Mad Dog' has been 'applied by others a great many times upon man and beast and always with success'. If you use Snail

Water you 'must not expect any surprising good effects from it in the first month you drink it but have patience ... it has recovered many that were given over by several eminent physicians ...' and those who use the Jesuit's cure for 'Obstructions and divers infirmities' are warned that if the first attempt fails 'take it a second time and you'll hardly fail of your wishes'. A cure that had made a fortune – 'four or five hundred a year' – for its inventor had to be effective. 'If you fail of a cure it will be owing to your neglect' for after all had it not 'cured the Reverend Doctor Green of Coleson in Wiltshire when his nerves were contracted.'

Margaret Jensen
Wiltshire, 1995.

SOUPS & SAVOURIES

Soup: strong decoction of flesh for the table.

Let the cook daub the back of the footman's new livery, or when he is going up with a dish of soup, let her follow him softly with a ladle-full. (Swift)
Johnson's Dictionary 1755

... I think everything passed off uncommonly well, I assure you. The dinner was as well dressed as any I ever saw. The venison was roasted to a turn – and everybody said they never saw so fat a haunch. The soup was fifty times better than what we had at the Lucas's last week; and even Mr Darcy acknowledged that the partridges were remarkably well done; and I suppose he has two or three french cooks at least.

Jane Austen: *Pride and Prejudice*

In the eighteenth century soups were not usually served as a separate course: it was customary to offer soup as one of several dishes which together made up the first course of a meal. John Farley in *The London Art of Cookery and Housekeeper's Complete Assistant* published in 1792 suggested a dinner menu for November in which the first course consisted of beef collops, fish, tongue, patties and chicken in addition to two kinds of soup, onion and chestnut.

Cock Broth
Take a brisk young cock, twist his neck as quick as you can and skin him before his blood cools. Take out his entrails and put him into a saucepan which you must have ready with an onion, a thin crust of bread and a blade of mace and as much cold water as will cover him. Then let the saucepan boil up once or twice then take

him out and break every bone of him. Cut his liver and gizzard small and let all simmer together for six hours upon a very slow fire. Care must be taken it don't boil over and you must be sure to preserve his blood by putting him into the saucepan as quick as you can after you have skinned him. It's a fine, light and strengthening broth for a weak or declining stomach also a great restorative.

A similar recipe is to be found in one of the earliest English cookery books *The Closet of the Eminently Learned Sir Kenelm Digby, Knight, Opened* published in 1669 where it is described as 'Queen Henrietta's Morning Broth' taken to ensure the queen's continued health.

Fine Almond Hogs' Puddings

One pound of the finest white stale bread grated and sifted, one pound of Naples biscuits grated and half a pound of Jordan almonds pounded not too small, the peels of two lemons sheered very fine, a pound and a half of kidney beef suet cut very fine, a little beaten mace, ten eggs but half the whites. Beat them bur a little, wet it with warm sweet cream. Let it be no stiffer than butter, sweeten it to your taste and don't fill your skins too full.

This is probably a more elegant and certainly more expensive dish than William Cobbett was thinking of when, in *Cottage Economy*, he mentions 'hog's puddings' when describing the killing of a small-holder's pig: The inwards are next taken out, and if the wife be not a slattern, here, in the mere offal, in the mere garbage, there is food, and delicate food too, for a large family for a week; and hog's puddings for the children, and some for neighbours' children, who come to play with them ...'

I imagine he would also have enjoyed the following dish since he is most enthusiastic about his own methods of geese-rearing:

I have had a good deal of experience with regard to geese ... for three years ... I have had the finest geese that I ever saw, or ever heard of ... the reader will be apt to exclaim, as my friends very often do, 'Cobbett's Geese are all Swans.'

Gooseblood Pudding

Take the crumb of two penny loaves grated, half a pound of beef suet cut very small, pepper, salt and nutmeg, a few sweet herbs and onions, a little pennyroyal and fennel. Mix all these together in the goose's blood with three eggs and tie it up tight. It must boil an hour.

A Pudding (or Stuffing) for a Hare's Belly

Take an equal quantity of grated bread and grated apple and a fourth part of grated onion with a little pepper and salt. Mix all these up with a bit of butter and melted butter for the sauce.

A Lorain Soup

Boil three chickens then cut them in pieces. Take all the white meat and pound it. Take three french rolls and cut off the crusts, four turnips and two onions. Cut the turnips, bread and onions in pieces, a bunch of sweet herbs, some whole pepper and salt with a blade of mace. Put all these in a stew pan with a piece of butter as big as an egg and keep it stirring until thoroughly hot. The same liquor you boil your chickens in put in your stew pan. Let it boil three hours very slowly keeping it skimmed then pick out all the bones. Rub it through a cheesecloth with the white of the chicken that you kept out. Heat it very hot but not to boil. The crust of the rolls cut in shapes as you please, fry in butter and put in the soup and a lamb's head or a sweetbread in the middle of the soup when you dish it up.

A Rice Amulet

Take half a pound of rice and boil it very well. When it is enough beat it in a mortar with two spoonfuls of flour. Break in four eggs with two whites only. Season it with salt, a little sugar, nutmeg and cinnamon then put in half a pint of milk or cream and fry it.

19

A Rice Soup

Take a leg of beef, put it to boil overnight. Season it with six onions, some salt and Jamaica pepper, cloves and mace. Be sure to skim it well before you put in the spices. This will make two large dishes of soup then strain it to take off the fat. Take some of the broth and put either a fowl or knuckle of veal to boil in it. Take a quarter of a pound of rice and boil it softly in some of this broth then put it to the fowl or veal. Put some well-seasoned clear gravy in it just as it is going up. It must not boil afterwards for fear of discolouring it. Put your fowl or veal in the middle of your soup.

VEGETABLES

Sow peasen and beans in the wane of the moon,
Who soweth them sooner he soweth too soon,
That they with the planet may rest and arise,
And flourish with bearing most plentiful wise.

Thomas Tusser 1524-80

The art of gardening having been so much studied and improved of late
years, it consequently has introduced such an amazing variety of foreign
vegetables for our tables and improved the common sorts, that it requires
many alterations and improvements quite different from the manage-
ment of gardens in former times; the difference of the seasons is now
scarcely to be known from the produce on our tables ...

Sir Richard Weston:
The Gardener's and Planter's Calendar, 1778

Although a wide range of vegetables was available to the eighteenth
century cook this manuscript contains very few recipes for cooking them.
Jane Grigson in her *Vegetable Book* explains that it was not until the
1760s that the term vegetable' came to mean 'herbs and roots grown for
food'. However, 'pot herbs' , carrots, onions and turnips, might be an
integral part of many dishes and recipes for meat and fish include
vegetable ingredients. In 1699 John Evelyn listed seventy-two varieties
of salad herbs and vegetables in his *Acetaria* and in 1778 Richard
Weston's treatise on gardening named eighteen varieties of peas, twenty-
seven varieties of beans, seventeen varieties of lettuce and six varieties
of broccoli as well as scorzonera, Hamburg parsley and cardoons in a
'catalogue of kitchen garden seeds and plants and their varieties' that
occupies eight closely printed pages. In 1747 Hannah Glasse in *The Art*

21

of Cookery Made Plain and Easy offered the following advice:

N.B. In your first Course, always observe to send up all Kinds of Garden Stuff suitable to your Meat etc. in different dishes, on a Water dish filled with hot Water on the Side Table ...

Although Cumberland sauce, apple sauce and redcurrant jelly remain as traditional accompaniments to meat the dividing line between sweet and savoury dishes has become more distinct of recent years. The manuscript contains many recipes which can be seen as part of a continuous tradition from the Middle Ages and earlier in which sugar and spices are added to savoury dishes and in which vegetables are used, as in the first three recipes in this chapter, as a basic ingredient for sweet dishes.

Artichoke Pie

Take the bottoms of four large artichokes, boil them very tender and take off all the black with care. Boil some vinegar and water together then put in your bottoms again. Let them boil a little and take them out and drain them. Cut them in square pieces and lay at the bottom of your pie then a layer of citron cut thin then a layer of pistachio nuts and so till your pie be almost full then stick it with large pieces of good marrow and lid your pie. When it comes out of your oven make a caudle with half a pint of white wine and the yolks of five eggs well beaten. Sweeten it well and pour it hot over your pie. Lay on the lid again and serve it up hot.

Carrot Fritters

(Take) three middling carrots boiled tender, pound them in a mortar then take half a pint of thick cream, three ounces of flour, three ounces of grated bread, four eggs well beaten, a little beaten mace and sugar to your taste. Mix all well together and fry them in butter or lard but be sure your liquor boils.

Carrot Pudding

Take a large carrot and grate it. Put it into a mortar with half a pound of sugar. Beat it pretty well then put in half a pound of butter and beat it very well. Grate it in four biscuits and put to it eight eggs with only four whites well beaten. Work all these together well, cover the bottom of your dish with puff paste and turn up the edges of the paste with a pinch. Draw a little fresh butter and put in the white of an egg and wash it all over then scrape some fine sugar over it and bake it for half an hour.

A modernised version of this recipe can be found in Jane Grigson's *Vegetable Book* substituting breadcrumbs for biscuit crumbs and flavouring the filling with orange flower water and brandy.

Mushroom Patties

Your mushrooms being fresh gathered pick, rub and wash them. Put them in a stew pan with a quarter pound of butter, a little thyme, parsley, pepper, salt, some little slice of bacon stuck with cloves and a whole onion. Cover it close and let it stew over a slow fire. Shake in a little flour and give them a shake now and then as they stew that they do not turn. When your liquor comes to be as thick as cream. Throw out the onion and the bacon. set it by to be cold. Sheet a little patty pan with thin puff paste. Put in your mushrooms and a little juice of lemon. Cover your patty. It will be ready as soon as the crust is baked.

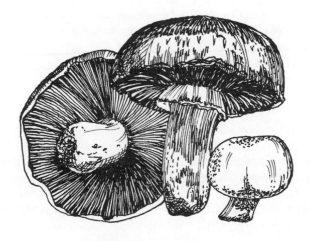

In 1699, the same year that John Evelyn published his *Acetaria*, William King wrote in his *Journey to London* of the English suspicion of mushrooms:

I desired to know what Mushrooms they had in the Market. I found they had but few, at which I was surpris'd, for I have all my life been very

Curious and inquisitive about this kind of Plant, but I was absolutely astonish'd to find, that as for Champignons, and Moriglios [morels], they were as great strangers to 'em as if they had been bred in Japan'.

Stewed Asparagus

Cut the tops and green of the asparagus as small as peas. Put it to stew in a little water with butter, thyme, winter savory, shredded onion, pepper, salt and cloves. When it is tender thicken it up with cream.

The recipe above seems to be a way of dealing with asparagus 'thinnings' rather than the best quality vegetable. The recipe which follows implies that in the eighteenth century truffles were more easily obtained – and cheaper – than they are today. Ralph Whitlock in *The Folklore of Wiltshire* gives an account of the history of truffle-hunting in Winterslow near Salisbury. The Winterslow truffle-hunters petitioned Parliament in 1860 in an attempt to have their dogs exempted from the annual dog tax on the grounds that they and their ancestors had for generation used dogs for their work '... being poor labouring men living ... where there is a great many English truffles grow, which we cannot find without dogs, we do therefore keep and use a small poodle sort of dog ... wholly and solely for that and no other ... '

Truffles – to use when raw

The truffles are first to be washed clean by rubbing them with a brush in warm water several times then put them in a pot with a bottle of burgundy, eight cloves, two or three blades of mace, three ounces of fat bacon, a little thyme, parsley and a bay leaf. Let them boil over a slow fire for an hour then take any quantity of them you want to use and put them into a sheet of writing paper first rubbed over with sweet oil. Put them into a sheet of brown paper and dip them into water and bake them in the hottest wood ashes you can get for a quarter of an hour then take them out and serve them up hot in a clean napkin.

MEAT & FISH

June 10 1668 So forth toward Hungerford led this good way by our landlord one Heart an old but very civil and well spoken man ... so came to Hungerford where very good trouts eels and crayfish dinner. A bad mean town.

The Diary of Samuel Pepys

Wednesday, 22 February – About four p.m. I walked down to Wylye. We played at brag the first part of the even. After ten we went to supper on four boiled chicken, four boiled ducks, minced veal, sausages, cold roast goose, chicken pasty and ham ... about three o'clock, finding myself to have as much liquor as would do me good, I slip't away unobserved, leaving my wife to make my excuse. Though I was very far from sober, I came home, thank God, very safe and well, without even tumbling; and Mr French's servant brought my wife home at ten past five.

Thomas Turner
The Diary of a Georgian Shopkeeper (1758)

And ye, fat eels and trout may feed
Where Kennet's silver waters toss
Proud are your Berkshire hearts to bleed
When drest with Goodman's prime Vale Sauce

Advertisement c.1840

Buttered Chicken

Take three good chickens and boil them enough then skin them and cut them in large pieces. Put them in your stew-pan with a little of the liquor you boiled them in and some sweet cream with half a nutmeg grated. Set it on the fire till it is thoroughly hot then pour in half a pound of butter melted. Squeeze in a large lemon and

25

toss it up shaking in a little flour to thicken it. Garnish your dish with lemon.

Buttock of Beef, Red

Take buttock of beef, dry it very well with a cloth and cut off the fat. Take two ounces of salt, pepper and two ounces of bay salt beat fine, half a pound of very coarse sugar. Rub it very well in both sides of the beef then salt it well with common salt and let it lie three weeks turning it sometimes. When you boil it bind it with tape to keep it in shape. It must boil very slow and till it is very tender. Eat it hot or cold.

The bay salt referred to here is coarse crystals of sea-salt obtained by natural evaporation. It was cheaper than 'fine salt' and more effective for preserving meat or fish.

Calves' Ears Forced

Take four calves' ears with the skin on, let them be well scalded and cleaned, put them in a pot of water, put to them a little fat bacon, mutton fat and two or three onions. Let them braise in this until tender. When done fill the ears with a light forcemeat, bind them up and roast them. Serve them up with a light cooley or a light ragout.
N.B. They make a pretty dish cut up in slivers tossed up in a light cooley or ragout. Lambs' tails sealed, larded and roasted with the ears fricasseed make a pretty dish.

Of the two other dishes made from a calf's head one, for brawn, dated back to medieval times when it was more often made from a pig's head and served at feasts and banquets. The second recipe is for a much later, more 'fashionable' dish.

Calf's Head like Brawn

Take a calf's head with the hair on it. Soak it in fair water twelve hours then boil it till the hair will come off it by scraping with the back of a knife or any other way you can get it off without tearing the skin. After it is clean from hair split the head as it is usually brought from the butcher's. Take out the tongue and brains then clean the insides and wash it in several waters. Close the two parts together and tie it up in a cloth. Let it boil till it's very tender and all the bones will come out. Be sure to keep the [head] whole. After it is boned take a knife and mix the meat well together. Lay it even then shake some pepper and salt and mix it with the meat.

Roll it up like a collar fast bound in a cloth or clap the two sides together in a cloth while it is hot. Put it in an earthen pan or round bowl with the cloth both over and under. Put a board that will go in the inside of the pot and put a Jack weight on it and let it stand all night. Take it out of the cloth and make a pickle of vinegar and salt and water and let it stand to be cold before you put in your brawn. It is very good.

Calf's Head a la Turtle

Take a Calf's Head with the skin and ears on (after scalding to get off the hair). Bone it clean then boil it about half an hour. Afterwards put it in a clean pail of water. When cold cut it across according to the course of the head about an inch long and half an inch thick. When so done put your meat in a large stew-pan, add to it about a pint of good veal broth or rather soup, half a pound of butter, about half a pint of Madeira wine then season it with allspice and a little cayenne pepper and with parsley, thyme, basil, sweet marjoram and onions. let your spice be beaten very fine, your herbs and onions minced very fine but separate. To this composition you may add two ox pullets, one pair of goose giblets well stewed, the yolks of six or eight bantam eggs boiled hard with some good force-meat balls.

N.B. The meat of the calf's head will require about three hours stewing in which time you must ply it gradually. Just before you take it up take the yolks of three or four hard eggs, pound them in a mortar, add to them a little of your stock or soup, strain them through a sieve into your meat. It will bring it to a proper consistency and a good colour.

27

This dish owes its description to the turtle soup which first made its appearance on fashionable tables in the mid-eighteenth century but which remained rare and expensive. Hannah Glasse included a recipe for Mock Turtle in the 1758 edition of her *Art of Cookery*: C. Anne Wilson in *Food and Drink in Britain* describes the dish as 'a calf's head, well-seasoned and stewed in strong mutton or veal gravy and a quart of madeira, and served in its soup in an empty turtle shell, if one could be procured'. Other recipes gave the instruction 'hachir' the meat, that is cut it into small pieces. From this the word 'hash' came to mean a dish containing finely chopped meat. Parson Woodforde, known through his diaries as a man inordinately fond of his food, records an elegant dinner on June 26 1792:

There were six people present and the full menu included boiled tench, pea soup, a couple of boiled chicken and pig's face, hashed calf's head, beans, roasted rump of beef with new potatoes etc. Second course: roasted duck and green peas, a very fine leveret roasted, strawberry cream, jelly, puddings etc. Dessert - strawberries, cherries and last year's nonpareils.

The manuscript includes many foreign recipes: Dutch Cakes and Dutch Wafers, French Blancmange, Patties, Puffs and Pie, Italian Collops, Lobster Lorain, Spanish Butter and Tamarind Fish the Indian Way. The following recipe, though it has no national attribution, is clearly an early version of the Greek dish Dolmades. Elisabeth Ayrton in *The Cookery of England* gives a very similar recipe, 'To Make a Delma (Dolmadis)' taken from Mrs Ann Blencowe's Receipt Book, first published in 1694.

Delmas

Take the lean of a loin of mutton and as much beef suet as for forcemeat. Shred them small, put the same quantity of rice boiled tender. Season it with suitable herbs, pepper, salt and a little nutmeg then mix it well together and break in one or two eggs according to the quantity of your meat. Then take cabbage or vine leaves and dip them in hot water. Fill them with your meat and roll them up like cucumbers. Tie them with coarse thread and put them in a stew pan with gravy. Cover them and let them stew gently over a slow fire till they are thoroughly done. Take them out of the thread and thicken your gravy with the yolk of an egg and pour it over them.

Hung Beef

Take six ribs of beef, young and fat, two ounces of saltpetre, four ounces of coarse sugar, four ounces of bay salt, two pounds of common salt. Mix all these together and rub it well into the meat. Let lie in the brine a fortnight often turned and rubbed over. Then take the same ingredients fresh and repeat the operation a fortnight more then hang it in a place dry, warm and airy till it is well dried and keep it afterwards in some airy place not too warm. It may be eaten after two, three or four months. In dressing soak it in water the night before you roast it. Baste it with boiling water a quarter of an hour before a good fire and continue basting with water now and then till it is enough which will be in less time than beef unprepared in this manner. It may be eaten hot or cold. From Sir John Shaw at Oxford. I think boiling it would be the preferable way of dressing it as it would be salt and hard.

Italian Collops

Take a piece of veal and cut it in very thin slices and beat it with the back of a knife. Take a saucepan and butter the bottom of it and lay in the collops. Have a bit of parsley and a little lemon peel chopped small and throw over them then season them with pepper, salt and a little nutmeg. Cover them close and set them over a slow fire. Turn them now and then that those at the top may be done enough. Add four spoonfuls of hot broth. Have some cream and the yolks of three eggs and shake amongst them until the sauce be thick. You may put a little onion if you like it. Squeeze in some lemon juice and serve it up.

Collops were originally thin slices of bacon which had been a popular dish, fried with eggs, since medieval times. By the eighteenth century the word collop had come to mean a thin slice of meat of any kind – and *Johnson's Dictionary* of 1755 gives as an additional usage 'collop ... in burlesque language, a child!'

Lobster Lorain

Take the meat of two lobsters. Mince it small with two anchovies and the yolks of three hard eggs, a little parsley and sweet herbs with a little pepper, beaten mace, cloves and nutmeg.
  Mix all these together well then have some french bread boiled

in cream, about four ounces of butter, the yolk of three eggs and the white of one. Mix these with the above ingredients then have some scallop shells well buttered and strewn with crumbs of bread. Fill them with the above meat and set them in the oven for half an hour. Beat the body of the lobster in a mortar very well and put them in a saucepan of water or broth and boil them a little while. Strain off the liquor and put to it a glass of sack and some butter and draw it up as thick as you can with some juice of lemon. Put your shells of lobster in a dish and pour the sauce all over them and send them up hot.

Lobster Pie

Make good paste and put it at the bottom of your dish then a layer of butter then the meat of three lobsters in as large pieces as you can. Season it with beaten mace, two or three cloves and salt. Shred two anchovies small with a little parsley. Mix all these together and strew it all over your lobster with a piece of good butter here and there and at last a layer of good butter on the top. When it goes into the oven put in a little water. Just when it comes out of the oven have ready a glass of claret with a little gravy thickened with the yolks of two eggs and a little juice of lemon. Put it into your pie.

Mr Quin's Sauce for Fish

Half a pint of old mushroom catchup, half a pint of old walnut pickle, six large anchovies pounded, six cloves of garlic, three pounded and three whole, cayenne pepper half a teaspoonful. Before you use it shake the bottle. To stand at the sideboard or mix what you like with melted butter for sauce.

The other fish sauce in the manuscript uses a base of one part of wine vinegar to two parts of red wine, flavoured with mace, cloves, black pepper, nutmegs, horseradish, onions, bay leaves, parsley and thyme. 'Ten anchovies washed, boil altogether an hour and a half till it comes to a pint. Bottle it for use. One large spoonful will be enough for half a pint of melted butter.'

Oyster Sausages

Take a pound and a half of the lean of a leg of mutton or inside of
Sir Loin of beef with a pound of beef suet. Shred both very fine.
Take a pint and a half of oysters, shred them but not small. Mix
the above with a little handful of sage chopped small with a very
little thyme. Mix all these together with the yolks of three eggs and
about four spoonfuls of the oyster liquor. Season it with pepper,
salt, mace and cloves. Make them up as you fry them in good
butter. Before you put your sausages to fry beat up the yolk and
white of an egg and dip your sausages in one by one and cover them
with grated bread. You must not fry them too hard.

This combination of fish and meat is one that began to be common in the
seventeenth century. Oysters, which could be bought for as little as two
shillings a hundred, were an inexpensive and frequently used ingredient
for pies or as part of a stuffing for duck, capon or a leg of mutton. Street-
sellers of oysters would attract customers with the cry:

> *Buy my Oysters, live Oysters, O!*
> *Twelve pence a pack, Oysters, O!*
> *My fine native Oysters,*
> *Fresh and fine are the best,*
> *For court and for cloisters,*
> *For yourselves or your guest.*

Although the recipe above is for a dish that is now unknown, during the
eighteenth century 'sausages' usually of chopped beef or mutton mixed
with oysters were a fashionable dish.

Paris Patties

Take a fowl and parboil it a little. Bone and skin it then shred it
extremely fine. Shred also half a pound of beef suet. Beat after
blanching half a pound of almonds with no more sack or orange
flower water than will keep them from oiling. Season it with salt,
nutmeg, cloves and mace with a little sugar. Mix it well together
then make some fine puff paste and cover the bottoms of your little
patty pans. put in some of these ingredients and lay on the top
some pistachio nuts blanched and some candied citron, orange
and lemon peel. Add little bits of marrow then lid your patties and
bake them.

Pickled Pigeons

Take twelve large fine pigeons. Bone them whole then season them by rubbing the insides with pepper, salt cloves and mace beaten small. Sew up or tie their joints and rumps with thread. Stuff them pretty full with spinach, lettuce and strawberry leaves, their own livers, a little thyme, parsley, winter savory, sweet marjoram, shallot, a little lemon peel, two cloves of garlic and twelve anchovies all shred very small. Put an equal quantity into each pigeon then tie up their necks tight and put them into two quarts of boiling water. Give them one boil then take them out and lay them one by one upon a dish till they be cool and the pickle cool likewise. Make the pickle. Put to the liquor you boiled them in a bunch of sweet herbs, a little whole pepper, mace and cloves, a pint of white wine, as much good vinegar and a clove or two of garlic. Some likewise put the bones. When all boils put in the pigeons and boil them in the pickle for about half an hour or until you think them enough. Take them up and when both pigeons and pickle are separately cold put them altogether in a pot or glass with a narrow mouth. Put two or three spoonfuls of sweet oil on top and tie them up close with leather. They will keep good nine months or longer. You must observe to skim them well in the boiling.

A Pig a la Daube

Take a pig and split him down the back. Cut him in six pieces. First cut off the head and slit it then have a stewpan just big enough to stew it in. Put with it salt, pepper, cloves and mace, a bunch of sweet herbs, an onion, a slice of lemon peel with four bay leaves and a quart of the best vinegar. Let it stand twenty-four hours and then put in a pint of water and if that don't cover it put in more vinegar. Set it over a gentle fire and stew it till it's tender. Serve it up either hot or cold.

This extremely vague recipe doesn't make it clear whether it is the whole pig or just the head being cooked. On reflection it would require a fairly small pig and a remarkably large stewpan.

Snipe a la Basilisk

Take twelve snipe with their heads on, make a forcemeat with a sweetbread and some french bread soaked in cream, a little thyme, marjoram, parsley and beef suet. Beat it well in a mortar with the yolks of two eggs and the white of one, a little salt, pepper and beaten mace. Cut another sweetbread in long pieces and cover them with the forcemeat then stuff your snipe with the pieces. Tie the ends close. Cover your snipe all over with fat bacon and put them into some strong broth. Let them stew but not too much. Take them out of the broth, take off the bacon and clean them well from the broth. Put them in some hot gravy and let them stew gently till the sauce is thick.

Elizabeth Hartley in *Food in England* explains that snipe were always cooked complete with 'heads, turning the long beak of the snipe sideways, to act as a skewer'. There are, however, no clues to the dish's puzzling title. Eighteenth century definitions of 'basilisk' include not only the legendary serpent whose look could kill but also a large brass cannon or the golden-crested wren!

To Pumeroy a Brace of Carp

Bleed your carp into half a pint of white wine. Take the livers of the carp, chop them fine with two anchovies, a handful of parsley, four single sprigs of thyme, a little bit of onion, two spoonfuls of elder vinegar, four corns of white pepper, beaten. Shake in a little flour. Put all these into a silver saucepan and let them stew gently about an hour. Put in three-quarters of a pound of butter, boil your carp and drain them very well. Put sippets about your dish and pour the sauce over them.

To Ragout a Breast of Veal with Peas

Let the veal be half roasted then take out all the short bones and put your veal in a ragout pan [stew pan] with strong gravy and stew it till it is tender. Season it to your taste. Thicken it with butter and flour mixed together. Fry your sweetbread in dice and throw it in with forcemeat balls and half a peck of green peas, boiled, and some mint small shred, and five or six spoonfuls of your pea liquor. Serve it up in a soup dish.

Half a peck of green peas is a little more than six pounds. Sir Richard Weston's Gardener's Calendar of 1778 lists eighteen varieties: advising that 'the early sorts' could be gathered 'from April to June' and 'the late sorts ... from June to November'.

To Stew Carp, Trout or Tench

Scale, clean and wash them well. Take a stew pan to the size of your fish, put them in and strew some young onions and parsley chopped fine over them. Bone two anchovies and stick a large onion with three or four cloves. Season it with salt, some peppercorns, a little mace and a bay leaf. Cover it with Rhenish or French white wine or any that is sharp (but Rhenish is best). Put them over a slow fire and when they are stewed enough take them up and drain them well. Put them in the dish you intend to serve them up in then set the liquor on the fire again and let it boil to the quantity you think will cover your fish. Put in a quarter of a pound of good butter with flour worked into it. Let it boil in the liquor till it's pretty thick then strain it hot over your dish.

Another slightly earlier recipe suggests a sauce of 'butter, grated bread, the juice of orange, cinnamon with currants; make them up into a sauce with herbs, and serve them up with green garnish'.

Tamarind Fish the Indian Way

Take twelve large hard-roed mackerel, cut off the heads and tails then slit them down the back and take out the bone. Clean them very well with a cloth but don't wash them. Salt them and let them lie twenty-four hours in that. Shift them from the bottom to the top then get six pounds of sour tamarinds, put them in some vinegar and work and break them with your hand till it's like a hasty pudding. Cut one of the fish into four pieces and rub it well over all the pieces. Lodge in a clean stone jar close together and the roes on the sides. Fill your jar and tie it close down with a bladder and leather. When you use them you must fry them in butter. They will keep three months.

The *Shorter Oxford Dictionary* defines Tamarind Fish as 'a relish made from various kinds of Indian fish preserved with the acid pulp of the tamarind fruit'.

The tree, *Tamarindus indica*, bears pods containing hard seeds surrounded by pulp.

To Cure Hogs' Faces

To eight faces take eight ounces of saltpetre, one pound of bay salt, one pound of very coarse sugar all well dried and powdered then mixed with common salt enough to cover them well. Let them lie in that eight days then take some bloody brine clarified well and dissolve bay salt and saltpetre in it till it will bear an egg high up. Boil and skim it well. When it is cold put it to your faces and let them lie eight days more then dry them in a malt house. They are very good.

SWEET & SAVOURY PRESERVES

I teach both fruites and flowers to preserve
And candie them, so Nutmeg, Cloves and Mace
To make both marchpane paste, and sug'red plate,
And cast the same in formes of sweetest grace ...
When crystall frost hath nipt the tender grape,
And cleane consum'd the fruits of every vine,
Yet heere beholde the clusters fresh and faire,
Fed from the branch, or hanging on the line.

Sir Hugh Plat
Delightes for Ladies, 1600

Although the original manuscript contains a few savoury preserves the majority of recipes under this heading are for the use and preserving of familiar fruits: apples, apricots and peaches, cherries, red and white currants, damsons, plums, raspberries and gooseberries. Many of the recipes, for fruit pastes and jellies would produce dry, solid conserves which would have excellent keeping qualities

Apricot Paste

Pare and stone two pounds of apricots, strew on them one pound of sifted sugar and let them stand till that is melted then set it on the fire and boil it very fast mashing them as they boil very small. put to it a quarter of codlin jelly and boil it together very well. To a pound of your pulp put a pound and a half of sifted sugar. Let your pulp boil and shake in your sugar and only let it scald after the sugar is put in. Put it into little pots in your store and turn it out as other pastes and dry it.

Apple Jelly for All Sorts of Sweetmeats
Take two dozen of large codlings, pare, core and throw them into cold water as you do them to keep the colour. Then put into your pan as much water as you think will just cover your apples and make it boiling hot. Put in your fruit and boil as fast as you possibly can. When the apples are broke pour on them a quart or three pints of boiling water and let it boil till it is a strong jelly. Pour it through a flannel jelly bag. In summer codlings are best, in September Golden Rennets, in winter pippins or John apples.

The English taste for strongly flavoured, highly spiced food was given fresh impetus after the foundation of the East India Company so that by the eighteenth century curries, pickles and chutneys were appearing in the recipe books. The word 'catchup' or 'catsup' was first used in 1690, becoming 'ketchup' in 1711. It may possibly have developed from 'caveach' or 'cavitch', a highly flavoured marinade for meat or fish. Dr Johnson defines ketchup as 'a kind of pickle made from mushrooms'. The manuscript offers two such sauces which could be stored, as well as a recipe for cavitch:

Cavitch
Take one quart of vinegar, put to it ten large cloves of garlic, one quarter of an ounce of coriander seeds bruised, one dram of saffron. Let these ingredients stand till you think it strong enough then strain it off for use.

Catchup
Take a stewpan full of large flaps of mushrooms and the tips. Wash and rub them clean with salt as for pickling. Set it on a slow fire – be sure to dry them well before you set them on the fire. Put in a handful of salt. They will make a great deal of liquor. Strain it through a thin flannel bag. To two quarts of liquor put in half a pound of shallots, two cloves of garlic, some pepper, ginger, cloves, mace and a bay leaf. Boil it and skim it. When it is quite cold put it into bottles and stop it very close.

Catchup the Indian Way
Take a gallon of strong beer, half a pound of anchovies clean washed and picked, a quarter of an ounce of mace, a quarter of an

ounce of pepper, three large roots of ginger, half a pound of shallots, one quart of flap mushrooms well rubbed and picked. Set it on a slow fire close covered. Let it boil till it's half wasted then drain it through a flannel bag. When it is quite cold put it into very dry bottles and stop it very close.

It is thought to be the most agreeable taste and relish to fish sauce that can be.

Cherry Jam

Take twelve pounds of Kentish cherries. Stone and put them into a preserving pan. Set them over the fire, break and mash them as they boil till all the juice is gone and the cherries are dry and the stuff will come from the bottom of the pan. Take it off the fire and put in three pounds of fine sifted sugar, mix it well together then set it on the fire again. Let it have a boil or two then put it into flat pots or china cups.

By the end of the eighteenth century 'cowcumbers' had become cucumbers but the manuscript retains the old spelling. Jane Austen, writing from Bath to her sister Cassandra, speaks of cucumbers costing a shilling and being 'a very acceptable present'. The Chelmsford Chronicle carried a report of one particularly impressive specimen on October 20 1779:

A cucumber was lately cut in the garden of Henry Shuttleworth Esq. of Great Bowden, near Market Harborough, Leicestershire, which measured in length thirty-one inches, was three feet eleven inches over the middle, and weighed sixty pounds.

Unfortunately it seems likely that this epic vegetable was in fact a marrow, the two names being interchangeable at the time.

Cowcumbers Preserved

Take cucumbers of the same bigness you would for pickling. Let them be picked fresh and green and free from spots. Boil them in water till they are tender then run a knitting needle the long way through them and scrape off the roughness. Green them thus. Let your water be ready to boil, take it off and put into it a good handful of beaten alum. Set it on the fire and put in the cucumbers. Cover them very close till you see they look green. Weigh them and take their weight in single refined sugar and a pint of water to a pound of sugar. Boil your syrup, put in your cucumbers and boil them a little close-covered. Set them by and boil them a little every day for four days then take them out and make a syrup of a pound of sugar and half a pint of water to every pound of cucumbers. Put in your cucumbers and boil them till they are clear. Put in the juice of two lemons and a little orange-flower water. Give it a boil all together. You may lay some of them out to dry or keep them in the syrup but every time you take any out you must make the rest scalding hot or they will work (i.e. ferment).

Currants Dried in Bunches

When your currants are stoned and tied up in bunches take to a pound of them a pound and a half of sugar and half a pint of water. Boil your syrup very well then lay your currants into your syrup and set them on the fire. Let them just boil then take them off and cover with a paper. Let them stand till next day then make them scalding hot but do not boil. Let them lie in the syrup three or four days with a paper close to them. Lay them on china or earthen plates and sift them well with sugar. Put them into a store and the next day put them on (their) sides but do not turn them till that side is dry. Turn them and sift them with sugar on the other side and when they are dry lay them in a box with paper between.

Dried Angelica

Take the stalks of angelica, boil them tender, let them drain and scrape off all the thin skin. Put them into scalding water and cover them close. Set them over a slow fire to be very green but don't let them boil. Drain them very well and put them into a very thick syrup of the weight and a half of sugar. The syrup must be well boiled and stand to be cold before you put in the angelica. Warm it every day till it is very clear then lay it on glass to dry sifting some fine sugar over them. You may keep some in the syrup.

Instructions for making 'clear cakes' of apricots, red and white currants, lemons, oranges, quinces and raspberries are given in detail. For some of these there are also instructions for making the fruit into paste or cakes for storage.

Gooseberry Clear Cakes

Take a gallon of white gooseberries and wash them. Put to them as much water as will cover them all over, set them on a hot fire and let them boil a quarter of an hour or more. Run it through a flannel jelly bag. To a pint of liquor have ready a pound and a half of sifted fine sugar. (Pour) through a hair sieve, set the jelly over the fire and let it boil up. Shake in the sugar stirring it all the while the sugar is putting in. It must be taken off the fire to put in the sugar and directly set on again. Let it scald till the sugar is melted but by no means boil. Lay a thin strainer of canvas on a flat dish and pour your jelly through it. Turn back your strainer by degrees to take off the scum. Fill it as fast as you can into little flat pots or glasses then set them into your store to dry. When they are candied on the top turn them out onto a glass to dry. When very dry on one side turn the other. Twice turning is enough. If any stick to the glass hold them a little over the fire and they will come off. A gallon of gooseberries will make but three wine pints of jelly.

Lemon (or Orange) Clear Cakes

Make a very strong pippin jelly. Run it through a jelly bag and the meat of four either oranges or lemons which you design making, boil them together and rub it through the sieve again. Take a quarter of a pound of sugar, just let it boil then to a pint of the jelly put half the syrup of the fruit and the rind of one pared and boiled in two or three waters and shred very fine. Make them scalding hot together. To a pint of the above jelly so mixed take a pound and half of sugar, put a little water to it but don't beat it. Boil it to a candy then put in but half your jelly to the hot sugar. As soon as it has done boiling put in the rest and set it over the fire till all the sugar has melted. Take care it does not boil then fill it in little pots and turn it as other clear cakes.

41

And for comparison:

Orange Cakes
Pare off the outside rind of twelve Seville oranges then cut them in half and squeeze the juice and pulp into a basin. Boil the oranges very tender. You must shift them three times in boiling. When you take them out of the water dry them very well with a cloth and pound them fine in a mortar. Put to a pound of orange a pound of sugar but let your sugar be very dry. Mix them well together and let it be hot through. Put in your juice and pulp with the juice of six lemons, let all just boil and stir it about till it's almost cold. Drop it upon papers and set them in the sun or by the fire to dry. They will be a week a-drying.

Orange Drops
Take twelve seville oranges, cut them and squeeze out the juice. Boil the rinds very tender. Cut out most of the white and beat the yellow parts of the rinds very tender and rub through a hair sieve. Pick out all the seeds and skins and put it to your other pulps. Mix it well together. To a pound of the pulp put a pound and a half of sugar sifted through a hair sieve. Stir it well in the pulp and put in as much juice as you think will make it thin enough to drop from a teaspoon upon glass. Set it by the fire and let it stand about two hours then put them into your stove. They will be dry in twenty-four hours. Some put only the pulp of the rinds but I have done them with some of the meat mixed and like it better.

Red Marmalade
Pare some quinces, quarter and cut out all the hard core. To a pound of quince a pound and a quarter of sugar and half a pint of the juice of barberries. Boil the barberries. After you have pounded them in a mortar put them into a little boiling water with a few black bullace [a type of round damson]. Boil it and run it through a jelly bag. Boil your quince, sugar and juice very slowly and let your pan be close covered. Stir it sometimes and boil it till it is very clear and tender. Put it into flap pots. (The bullace make it a fine colour).

Peaches Preserved in Brandy

Take two dozen of Newington peaches. Have ready a pan of boiling water and put in your peaches. Let them boil till they are tender and soft. Put them on a sieve to drain. Make a syrup of two pounds of sugar and three quarts of water, boil it and let it stand a little then put in the peaches and let them boil very slow a little while. Take them out and drain them.

Weigh your fruit and to every pound a pound and a half of sugar with half a pint of water to every pound and a half of sugar. Boil your syrup and skim it well then put in your peaches and boil very gently till the syrup is very thick. Set them by in the syrup till the next day then make another fresh syrup of four and a half pound of sugar to a pint and a half of water. Boil and skim it till it is very thick. Let it stand to be cold then pour into it a pint of right French Brandy. Drain your peaches well from their syrup and put them into the brandy syrup in a glass jar. Let the jar be close stopped with a cork and tied down with a leather.

Pomegranate Clear Cakes

Make a strong pippin jelly and run it through a jelly bag. Take a pint of your jelly and slice a lemon rind and all into it. Run it again through your bag then colour it as you like. To a pint of jelly put half a quarter of a pint of orange syrup. Make it as for orange clear cakes and let it have a boil together. Take a pound and a half of sugar and boil it to a candy with a little water. Put a little of your jelly at a time into your candy (about half) and when your candy has done boiling put in the rest of your jelly and scald it till the sugar is melted. Be sure not to let it boil. Pour it through a strainer to take off the scum into a broad dish. Fill it into little pots and set it in your stove to dry as other clear cakes.

The colour is made thus: take as much carmine as you can have for half a crown. Put to it two ounces of fine sugar and as much water as will wet it. Give it a boil and run it through a piece of muslin.

It is quite a disappointment to find this recipe totally free of pomegranates. The title seems to refer only to the colour that would have been produced by the addition of what was clearly a very expensive colouring agent, carmine.

To Dry Figs

Take six pounds of figs (the white ones are the best). Let them be not too ripe. Have a pan of boiling water ready, put in the figs and boil them until they are tender then drain and peel them with ease. Make a syrup with five pounds of sifted sugar and a quart and half a pint of water. Boil your syrup and skim it well. Let it stand to be almost cold then lay in your figs and boil them till they are clear and tender. Put them into an earthen dish and the next day scald them. So do for three days. Let them lie in the syrup for three days. When you lay them out to dry clear them from the syrup a little with your finger or else they will candy too much. Put them into your stove and turn them every day. Put them into a box with paper betwixt them.

To Dry Grapes

Take the large Bell grapes just before they are ripe, stone them in bunches and put them into scalding water. Cover them close with vine leaves and cover the pan keeping them in a scald by putting them on and off the fire till they are green. Give them a boil in the water then drain them on sieves and to every pound of grapes make a thick syrup of a pound and a half of sugar and half a pint of water. Let it stand to be cold then put in the grapes and scald them every day (but never let them boil) till the syrup is very thick. Let them stand a day or two in the syrup then lay them out on earthen plates and sift them with fine sugar. Dry them in a stove and when dry on one side turn them and sift them on the other side and dry them not too dry.

To Pickle Barberries

Pick out the fairest bunches of your barberries then take the rest of them and boil in salt and water strong enough to bear an egg for half an hour or more. Lay your fairest branches into a pot and when the liquor is cold pour it over them.

To Pickle French Beans

Take them before they are old and boil them tender then put them into pickle made with vinegar, salt and spice.

To Pickle Oysters

Take your great oysters. In opening save the liquor, wash them clean in it and strain it from the dross. Add some white wine and white wine vinegar, whole pepper, quartered nutmeg, mace and a little ginger with a few bay leaves. When the liquor is boiled almost enough put in your oysters and plump them. Lay them out to cool and when the pickle is cold pour it over them in a gallipot or barrel and keep them from the air.

To Pickle Walnuts

Take five hundred of large walnuts towards the latter end of July, rub them with a flannel and salt then run a knitting needle through the long way of the nut. Put them into a stone jar as you do them and let the jar be above three parts full then make a pickle of salt and water strong enough to bear an egg. Be sure to boil as much as will cover your walnuts. Pour on the pickle boiling hot and stove them down close with a coarse flannel and a brickbat on. Do so for ten days making a fresh pickle every day but do not make your pickle quite so strong as at first. The eleventh day drain them well in a large sieve and wipe them lightly with a flannel. As you put them into the jar strew in three pints of mustard seeds, three large handfuls of cloves of garlic. When you have almost filled your jars cover them thick with vine leaves. Make your pickle of half white wine vinegar and half rape vinegar. Boil it and pour it boiling hot on your walnuts. Stove them down for two days then cover your jars with bladder and leather and tie them down very close. Untie them in a fortnight and if they want pickle boil some vinegar and let it stand to be cold before you fill them up.

To Preserve Grapes

Peel and stone the grapes. Put them in a pan and cover them very close. Let them boil and sometimes set them off and on the fire till they are very green. Drain all the juice from them and to a pint of grapes put a pound and a half of sugar and half a pint of apple jelly. Let them boil very fast till they are clear and jelly very well then put them into pots or glasses with papers close to them.

To Preserve Raspberries

Take the juice of red and white raspberries. If you have no white raspberries use half codlin jelly. Put it through a jelly bag. Put two pounds of sugar to a pint and a half of the juice. Boil it and skim it well then put in three quarters of a pound of large ripe raspberries. Let them boil very fast a little while till you think they look clear. Put the raspberries into the pot first then strain the jelly to them to take out the seeds. When you put them into the pots stir them a little that the raspberries may not lie on the top.

Raspberries were originally an 'import' from France and a relative newcomer to English gardens, not being grown here until the middle of the sixteenth century.

To Preserve Seville Oranges with the meat in them

Take twelve large thick rind oranges and either rasp or pare them which you can best do. Cut out a round piece at the stalk end and keep the pieces. With a little scoop take out all the seeds but keep in the pulp as well as you can. Hold them against the light to see that all the seeds are out and put your scoop close to the sides for it is there you find most seeds. Throw them into cold water as you do them. Let them lie four days shifting the water every day. Put them into a pot of boiling water and boil them very fast. Shift them with boiling water two or three times as you boil them till they are very tender and the bitterness out. Lay them out on a sieve with the holes downwards to drain. Weigh them and take their weight in sugar and one pound more. Put half a pint of water to every pound of sugar. Boil it well and skim it. Put in your oranges and boil them fast and turn them often to preserve the colour. Boil them till they are very tender and very clear. Put them into a deep earthen dish with the holes upwards. Pour your syrup on them. You must let them stand ten or twelve days. Fill them up with the syrup two or three times a day and they will grow transparent clear in that time. Then take half a hundred of John apples or Golden Russets and make four quarts of apple jelly. Boil it as quick as you can. Run it through the jelly bag. To every quart of jelly put two pounds of fine sifted sugar. Boil your jelly very well and skim it well. Put your oranges and syrup into a preserving pan and make them scalding hot then pour your jelly boiling hot on them. Boil them very quick and skim them. Put in the juice of four large lemons and the juice of two large oranges. Make it hot before you put it in and just before you take it off the fire pare a thick rind seville orange very thick and boil it with your oranges. Put your oranges into your pots with the holes upwards. Split some skewers and lay them on your oranges to keep them down in your pots which must be filled very full with the jelly for they will sink a great deal. Put the points in the sides of the pots till you serve them up. They are very fine and will keep two years. Be sure to let your pots be boiled and dried a week before you use them. Don't let them stand on their bottoms to dry but on their sides.

To Sugar All Sorts of Small Fruit

Beat the white of an egg and dip the fruit in it. Let it lie on a cloth that it may not be too wet then take some sifted fine sugar and roll the fruit in it till it is quite dried and covered with sugar. Lay it on sieves to dry in a store or before the fire. It will keep good a week.

Walnuts Preserved

Take your walnuts and boil them in fair water and as you see the water grow black change it six or seven times. The waters must be scalding hot when you change them. When they are tender peel them and put them into sugar as you do them. Then put them into syrup. When they have boiled a while stick them with cinnamon and cloves. There must be their own weight in sugar properly made into syrup.

BREAD, CAKES & BISCUITS

As to the act of making bread, it would be shocking indeed if that had to be taught by the means of books. Every woman, high or low, ought to know how to make bread. If she do not, she is unworthy of confidence and, indeed, a mere burden on the community ... if I were a labouring man I should prefer teaching my daughters to bake, brew, milk, make butter and cheese, to teaching them to read the Bible till they had got every word of it by heart ...

William Cobbett
Rural Economy

I have never quite liked baker's bread since I saw a great heavy fellow in a bake-house in France kneading bread with his naked feet! His feet looked very white to be sure: whether they were that colour before he got into the trough I could not tell. God forbid that I should ever suspect that this is done in England!

ibid.

Though the manuscript includes recipes for numerous cakes and 'biskets' the writers seem to have agreed with Cobbett that there is little need to teach 'the making of bread' in books. There is virtually nothing about bread apart from a recipe for French Bread and a few passing references to 'penny loaves'. To compensate there are plum cakes, seed cakes, four kinds of gingerbread, cakes with almonds, saffron and a variety of other spices, cheesecakes, jumbles, and nearly a dozen kinds of biscuit and wafer.

Almond Cakes

Take half a pound of Jordan almonds. Blanch them and beat them very fine with four spoonfuls of rose and orange flower water. Take

49

the yolks of eight eggs well beat and four of the whites whipped to a froth. beat together then by degrees shake in threequarters of a pound of fine sugar and three spoonfuls of flour. Beat it with a whisk all the while the oven is heating. Just before you put it into the oven rasp in the rinds of three lemons and lastly put in the almonds and break them in a little. Bake them in little round pans buttered. Fill them but half full. They will be soon baked. Turn them out presently.

Note that all flour used for cakes must be well dried and cold again before you use it or the cakes will be heavy.

Almond Cheesecakes

Steep half a pound of almonds all night in cold water then blanch and beat them in a stone mortar with a spoonful of orange-flower or rose water, half a pound of loaf sugar beat and sifted, six ounces of butter melted and cold. Mix all these together and put in the yolks of four eggs and the white of one and a half then beat all together for half an hour. Don't fill your pans too full. Beat the other whites of eggs to a froth, spread the froth with a feather on the top of your cheesecakes and sift them over with fine sugar. Bake them in a hot oven.

C. Anne Wilson in *Food and Drink in Britain* notes that by the middle of the seventeenth century 'some cheesecakes contained neither cheese nor curds but instead a rich custardy mixture of eggs, butter, flour and unrenneted cream, duly sweetened and spiced' and that 'a further development a few decades later was the lemon cheesecake ... its filling was what we now call lemon cheese or lemon curd'.

Almonds had been a popular ingredient in English food since the Middle Ages. They were believed to be a cure for insomnia, dysentery and head-aches. Almonds could be used as a protection against witchcraft and, possibly most useful of all, it was thought that five almonds taken before drinking would prevent a hangover.

Apricot Jumbals

Coddle the fruit very tender, set their pulp in a dish to dry over a stone till next day then beat it and put as much fine sugar as will make it into a stiff paste. Colour it with cochineal or what you will. Roll it to your fancy and tie them in knots (and) so dry them.

The *Shorter Oxford English Dictionary* suggests that the name of these cakes may derive from gimmel or knot rings. These were given as love-tokens as in the poem by Robert Herrick.

> *Thou send'st me a true-love knot, but I*
> *Return a ring of gimmmels to imply*
> *Thy love had one knot, mine a triple tie.*

An earlier manuscript cookery book, that of Rebecca Price, written in 1681 included nine recipes for 'jumbells' adding to those flavoured with orange, lemon and almonds the particularly intriguing 'jumbells like trees: my Aunt Rye's receipt' which were coloured red, yellow, green and blue with flower and vegetable juices.

Bath Buns

Take half a pound of flour, mix it with eight eggs both yolks and whites and four spoonfuls of good yeast. Let it lie by the fire twelve minutes and in that time rub one pound of butter into one pound of flour cold then mix both together. Put into it a pound of sugar, caraway seeds and sprinkle a few over the buns. Let them stand on the tin plates by the fire a little while to make them rise before you put them in the oven.

Bath Water Cakes

Three pounds of fine flour well dried, a quarter of a pound of good butter well rubbed into the flour, a quarter of a pound of fine sugar, one ounce of caraway seeds. Wet it with new milk, mix it well together and roll it out as thin as possible. You can cut them out with any round thing and prick them all over as much as you can or else they will blister. Bake them on tin plates in a coolish oven.

These are really biscuits rather than cakes but both recipes would benefit from the association with Bath which, during the eighteenth century developed into England's most elegant spa, providing a 'cure' for some and a fashionable social scene for others. The caraway seeds that are common to both recipes were frequently used in the form of 'caraway comfits' as an antidote to indigestion.

In January 1756 the *Bath Advertiser* carried news of a 'Two Days Flying Machine', a London to Bath stage-coach service 'three times every fortnight, Monday and Friday one week, and Wednesday the next' for a cost to passengers of 'eighteen shillings each, and those on the outside at ten'.

A Biscuit Cake

To every five ounces of flour well dried put six ounces of double refined sugar broke in lumps and five eggs. Put the sugar to the eggs and beat them an hour and a half till they are light and grow thick. Put in all the flour and stir it together but be sure you don't beat it. Put in a lemon peel cut small. Butter the pan – an hour will bake it. Put it in the oven when brown bread comes out.

Buns

Take three pounds of flour, six or seven spoonfuls of yeast and a pint of milk. So knead it together as you do bread then cover it with a cloth and set it before the fire for a quarter of an hour. Take a pound of fresh butter and work it in the paste. Put in a pound of caraway comfits then make it up as fast as you can. Put a cross on each with a knife and flour your papers. This quantity will make thirty or forty.

A very similar recipe can be found in *The Experienced English House-keeper* by Elizabeth Raffald published in 1782. Describing them as 'Bath Cakes' she recommends that they 'be sent in hot for breakfast'.

Coriander Seed Cake

One pound of fine sugar sifted, five eggs (but three whites), four spoonfuls of orange flower water, two of rose and two of fair water. Beat this together for one hour then put in a pound of flour well dried and one ounce of coriander seeds soaked in elder vinegar for two hours. Just beat this together then make them in small cakes. Bake them in a slow oven for they must look white.

Curd Puffs

A gallon of milk – set it with rennet. When there is a tender curd drain it well from the whey then beat it in a mortar. Add to it eight eggs, three Naples biscuits, of flour and stale bread one handful. Beat it all together in the mortar with a little orange flower water till it is very light then make coffins of fine writing paper. Be sure to pin them fast, butter them and fill them but half full. Put them in a brisk oven for half an hour. When you send them up make a sauce of melted butter, sack and sugar and pour it over them.

The Naples biscuits mentioned here were thin, crisp biscuits made of sugar, eggs and flour, sometimes flavoured with rosewater. They were an ingredient of many sweet dishes or eaten with syllabubs, fruit-flavoured creams and jellies.

Chocolate Puffs

Take a pound of sifted sugar, eight ounces of chocolate grated and sifted through a hair sieve. Make it up into a paste with the whites of eggs whipped into a froth then beat it well in a mortar. Make it up into lumps or any form you like. Bake them in a cool oven on papers.

Chocolate was first imported to England in the middle of the seventeenth century. Samuel Pepys' diary records his use of chocolate 'to settle the stomach' and by the end of the century it was a popular breakfast drink as well as an ingredient in a variety of recipes. The first English factory for the processing of cocoa beans was opened, in Bristol, in 1728. Chocolate must have been one of the most expensive ingredients available to the eighteenth century cook: it had been heavily taxed since

1724 and its price by the 1760s was in the region of ten to fifteen shillings a pound. The manuscript includes two other chocolate recipes, for chocolate almonds and chocolate cream as well as suggesting its use as a colouring:

Chocolate Almonds

Take two pounds of sugar, half a pound of chocolate grated and sifted through a hair sieve, a grain of musk, a grain of amber, two spoonfuls of ben [probably benjamin i.e. benzoin]. Make this up to a stiff paste with gum dragon [tragacanth] steeped well in orange flower water. Beat it well in a mortar, make it in moulds like almonds and lay them on paper in a warm place to dry but not in a stove or oven.

Dutch Wafers

Take five eggs and half the bigness of a nutmeg of loaf sugar, beat these to a froth then put in three quarters of a pound of melted butter and a pint of milk which must be boiled and almost cold and three quarters of a pound of flour and three spoonfuls of yeast. Mix these well together and cover it with a cloth and set it before the fire for three hours and stir it every quarter of an hour. When you begin to bake your wafers you must put in a chocolate cup of fair water. You must butter your irons but once. Send beaten cinnamon with powdered sugar up with them.

Another recipe, for Brown Wafers, is much closer to a modern recipe for waffles although the final shape would be similar to a brandy snap. It omits the yeast from a mixture of milk, cream, eggs and flour with a spoonful of sack and the rind of a lemon. After baking on 'wafer irons ... over a charcoal fire till they are brown turn them over your fingers round and lay them in an earthen dish.'

Wafers have a long and respectable place in the history of English food. In the sixteenth century the court had a 'wafery' superintended by the Royal Waferer. Cardinal Wolsey, not content with annoying Henry VIII in a variety of other ways, needed two waferers for his own establishment. An older name for Mothering Sunday is Wafering Sunday. At fairs and festivals wafers were sold in the streets. Some were embossed with religious motifs or moral quotations.

It seems that both English and Dutch Wafers and wafer irons were exported to America to return as waffles. Doris E. Farrington in her collection of Early American recipes *Fireside Cooks and Black Kettle Recipes* includes an eighteenth century waffle recipe with the note that in Pennsylvania 'waffle irons, made in cast iron moulded into the shapes of hearts, tulips or the intertwined initials of the couple were a favourite gift for the bride-to-be'.

French Bread

Take half a bushel of fine flour, ten eggs and one pound and a half of fresh butter. Put in as much yeast as you do into manchet. Temper it with new milk pretty hot and let it lie half an hour to rise. Make it into rolls or loaves and wash it over with with an egg beaten in milk. Let not your oven be too hot.

When Catherine Morland visited Northanger Abbey her head was full of romantic fears and fantasies, the effect of reading – and believing – too many sensational Gothic novels. Jane Austen makes it clear that Catherine gave her mother cause for concern:

I hope my Catherine, you are not getting out of humour with home, because it is not as grand as Northanger ... you should always be contented, but especially at home because there you must spend the most of your time. I did not quite like at breakfast, to hear you talk so much about the French bread at Northanger.

Northanger Abbey

French Puffs

Take some warm water and strew in flour by degrees till it's a very thick paste. Boil it and keep it from lumps then put it in a marble mortar while it is hot and beat it as fast as you can till it is mixed. Put in twelve eggs but two whites. Put them in whole two at a time beating still till it is light that it will draw up. Then put it upon the bottom of a plate or dish. Make your lard boiling hot and draw them off with the head of a key and fry them but not too brown. When they are done put them upon paper in a sieve to drain. Sift them well over with sugar and send them in hot.

Fruit Biscuits

Scald the fruit, dry it well from the water and rub it through a hair sieve. Stir it in a pan over a fire till it is dry, the stiffer the better. Then take two pounds of sifted sugar, a spoonful of gum dragon very well steeped and strained and about a quarter of a pound of the same fruit. Mix it well with the sugar, beat it with a biscuit beater. Take the whites of twelve eggs beaten to a froth. Put in but a little at a time still beating till all is in and that it looks as white as snow and very thick. Drop on papers, put into a cool oven and shut it up to make them rise.

Gingerbread

Take a quart of treacle, put to it a quarter of a pound of melted butter, an ounce of beaten or grated ginger, a large nutmeg, a quarter of a pound of sugar and flour enough to make it up into rolls. Put in a few caraway seeds.
Another:
Take one pound of treacle, half a pound of butter, melt them together and put them in a pan. Put to it an ounce and a quarter of ginger, an ounce of caraway seeds and an ounce of coriander seeds. Mix it with flour till it is a paste and bake it till it is hard quite through. You may add citron cut in small lumps if you like it.

Gingerbread Drops

Take a pound of flour well dried and cold. Rub in a pound of butter, put one ounce of beat ginger, one ounce of coriander seeds bruised, a quarter of a pound of loaf sugar beat, a quarter of a pound of citron cut in small lumps, one pound of treacle and a quarter of a pound of candied orange. Mix all these well together. Make it in little cakes or drops and bake them on tin plates.

Yorkshire Gingerbread

Take a gill of brandy and a gill of ale, a pound and a half of fivepenny sugar, one ounce of cinnamon, half a spoonful of beaten cloves, a pennyworth of beaten ginger and a pennyworth of saunders. Mix these well together, put them into a pan and let them boil. Take three pennyworth of old white bread grated. Let it be dried before the fire. When your things are boiled pour them upon your breadcrumbs and work them up scarce as stiff as paste. You must save a little of your cinnamon to sift upon your cakes. You may blanch a few almonds and cut them in. Make them into cakes and print them. Bake them hard.

Ginger was an important ingredient in English cooking throughout the Middle Ages. In 1471 Margaret Paston was writing to her son John asking him to buy sugar and dates and to find out the prices of 'pepper, cloves, mace, ginger and cinnamon, almonds, rice, galingale, saffron, raisins of Corinth ... send me the price of each of these and if it be better cheap at London than it is here, I shall send you money to buy with such stuff as I will have'.

Elizabeth David in *Spices, Salt and Aromatics in the English Kitchen* notes that 'by the fifteenth century the popularity of ginger must have been tremendous ... nearly every dish, meat, fish or fowl has the same or similar litany of spices (in which) ginger and saffron win out over the mace and cloves'.

In 1669 Samuel Pepys was eating 'gingerbread made in cakes like chocolate, very good, made by a friend' which may have resembled the first of the manuscript's recipes. This seems to be for an unbaked gingerbread which is very close to medieval recipes. These were based on breadcrumbs and might contain aniseed and cinnamon, sweetened with honey and moistened with wine. Different colours were produced by adding liquorice, saffron or saunders (a red colouring). Gingerbread 'fairings' were sold in the streets and there were even 'gingerbread fairs' in the South of England and the Midlands. In Bath gingerbread biscuits sold at the Candlemas Fair were known as 'valentines'. Jean Harrowven in *Origins of Rhymes, Songs and Sayings* quotes the following as a gingerbread-seller's street-cry:

> *Smiling girls, rosy boys,*
> *Come and buy my little toys;*
> *Monkeys made of ginger bread,*
> *And sugar horses painted red.*

Gingerbread 'monkeys' were not the only available novelty. Moulds could be very elaborate with different designs for different occasions. Georgian hostesses favoured moulds made with coats of arms or sporting scenes and expensive gingerbread was covered in gold leaf. Matthew Prior's poem of 1721, quoted by Zara Ground-Peace in her *Old Cookery Notebook* illustrates a particularly persuasive way of teaching children to read:

> *To master John the English Maid*
> *A Horn-book gives of Ginger-bread;*
> *And that the Child may learn the better,*
> *As he can name he eats the letter.*

Writing of a later time, the end of the nineteenth century, Alison Uttley in *Recipes from an Old Farmhouse* says 'Gingerbread men ... were still fashioned in old moulds ... mine dates back to the time of the Napoleonic Wars. It is a solid block of beech wood ... with seven designs cut and carved with intricate and delicate accuracy ... there is a farmer with his sheaf of corn and sickle, an admiral with a shock of hair and a tricorne hat, a marine with a sword, a little church with three windows and a tower, a bird on a tree, a basket of fruit and a sportsman'.

Perhaps the last word on gingerbread should be Shakespeare's:

An had I one penny in the world thou should'st have it to buy gingerbread.
Love's Labour's Lost

Until the seventeenth century cakes were 'iced' by being covered with sugar and then replaced in the oven to form a crust of melted sugar 'icing'. The following recipe shows an eighteenth century development.

Icing for Cakes
The whites of five eggs whipped up to a froth then put in one pound of double refined sugar sifted and three spoonfuls of orange flower water. Beat it with a knife all the while the cake is in the oven. When it comes out of the oven ice it all over both top and sides but don't set it in the oven again for it will dry better without.

Lemon Cheesecakes
Half a pound of Jordan almonds blanched and beat very fine in a mortar with orange flower water. Boil the peels of three lemons very tender (shift the water once) and beat them very fine. Beat the yolks of eight and the whites of four eggs and strain them. Melt

three-quarters of a pound of butter to oil and let it stand till almost cold. Stir it well into the stuff and sweeten it with fine sugar. Make fine crust for them very thin. Strew fine sugar over them as they go into the oven.

Nuns' Biscuits

Two pounds of loaf sugar beaten and sifted, half a pound of almonds beat very fine with the whites of six eggs. Put your sugar in a basin with the yolks of five eggs and when they are well mixed together stir in your almonds by degrees. Grate in the peel of a lemon or two and a little piece of candied citron. Let it be well stirred together then stir in a quarter of a pound of flour and fill it into long biscuit pans that are well buttered. Half fill and as you set them in the oven strew a little fine sugar over them and bake them quick shutting up your oven as they begin to colour on the top.

A recipe very similar to this one and described as 'The Nun's Bisket' can be found in a book published in 1723, *The Cook's and Confectioner's Dictionary* by John Nott.

Orange Biscuits

Take the white peels of twelve large oranges and boil them very
tender. Dry them in a cloth and take the weight of them in double
refined sugar. Boil it to a candy then put in the stuff which you
must bruise very well with a spoon and a little of the orange juice.
Set it in the fire till it be melted and scalding hot but not boiling.
Put it into little moulds made with paper. Set them in a stove to
dry and when they are so on the top turn them upon glass. They
will soon be dry.

Plum Cake

Seven pounds of fine flour well dried and cold, two pounds and a
half of butter worked into it then grate in two nutmegs, half an
ounce of mace, three drams of cloves beat and sifted, one pound of
powdered sugar. Take sixteen eggs but leave out four whites and
beat them well. Put a full pint and a half of ale yeast to them then
warm three pints of cream and when it is cool pour in as (much as)
will make it a batter. Beat one pound of almonds not too fine with
sack and orange flower water then put in one pound of candied
citron, lemon and orange. Put in more if you design it very rich.
Mix it well together then put in seven pounds of currants well
picked, washed and dried. Let it stand before the fire to rise a
quarter of an hour. Put a paste on the outside of the bottom of your
hoop. Before you put the cake into the hoop beat it well with a
pudding stick for an hour. Don't fill your hoop above three parts
full. Two hours and a half will bake it.

Another recipe for 'the Children's Plumb Cake' is similar apart from the
additional instruction to 'have ready standing by the fire about a gill of
white wine [and] near as much brandy' to add to the yeast. 'Little Plum
Cakes' were very simple affairs with a pound and a half each of flour and
currants to three-quarters of a pound of sugar, three eggs, twelve
spoonfuls of cream and a grated nutmeg to produce 'two dozen of cakes'.

Pound Cake

Take a pound of good butter and beat it with your hand till it comes
to a cream. Mix a pound of well dried flour and a pound of fine
sifted sugar together, half of it beat by degrees with your butter,
then ten eggs with five of the whites very well beat by a spoonful

at a time. Mix with them a spoonful or two of white rosewater and three pennyworth of French brandy. Beat in the other half of your flour and sugar and lastly a pennyworth of caraway seeds. Beat it till it goes into a hot oven. Let it stand near an hour in the oven and take it not out of the hoop till it's cold.

Ratafia Drops

Take half a pound of sweet almonds and a quarter of a pound of bitter almonds. Blanch them and dry them before the fire or in a stove. Beat them extremely fine and put in a little white of egg to keep them from oiling, a pound of double refined sugar well dried, beaten and sifted, four whites of eggs beat up to a snow. Make them into paste and into little drops and put them on paper. Bake them in a slow oven. Be sure your paste be not too moist.

Sponge Biscuits

Take eighteen yolks of fresh eggs with the whites of nine. Beat the yolks very well and whip the whites to a froth then beat them as well together. Put to them two pounds two ounces of sifted sugar. Have ready half a pint of water with three spoonfuls of rosewater boiling hot and as you beat the eggs and sugar put in the hot water a little at a time till it's all in. Then set the biscuit over the fire (it must be beat in a brass or silver pan) keeping it beating till it is so hot that you cannot hold your fingers in it. Take it off the fire and beat it till it's almost cold then put in a pound and a half of flour well dried and cold and the rinds of two lemons grated. Bake it in little long pans and don't fill them over half full. They must be buttered and go into a quick oven. As they go in sift a little fine sugar over them. They will be baked in less than a quarter of an hour. Turn your cakes out of your pans as soon as you take them out of the oven with the bottoms uppermost on a clean board to keep them from being heavy.

In 1710 *Royal Cookery or the Compleat Court Cook* was published. Its author, Patrick Lambe, had first been employed as a pastry cook in the court of Charles II and, subsequently, at the courts of James II, William and Mary and Queen Anne. For the last twenty years of his life Lambe's title was First Master Cook in the royal kitchen. His book established a new fashion so that in the years that followed many recipes published were described as being in 'Queen Anne's fashion'.

The recipe which follows uses an extraordinarily large number of eggs to one pound of flour as well as needing to be beaten for a very long time. Eric Quayle in *Old Cook Books* describes Lambe's recipes as being 'high-class cooking at its most extravagant, with no thought of the time and labour involved ... '

Queen Anne's Breakfast or the Savoy Biscuits

Take fifteen fresh eggs. Break fourteen of them into a clean wooden bowl leaving out seven of the whites and beat them well with two spoonfuls of rosewater. Put in a pound and a half of fine sifted sugar and beat it all the while the oven is heating. Just before you put it in the oven stir in a pound of fine flour dried and cold, and half a pound of caraways and the other egg you left out with and all. Butter some large pans and fill them but half full. Don't let your oven be too hot. Shut them up close and they will be baked in half an hour.

The Savoy are made the same way only leave out the seeds and drop them long upon papers and lay the papers upon tins and put them into a hot oven and bake them as fast as you can.

Rusks

Take four pounds of flour dried, two ounces of caraway seeds, almost half a pound of butter, half a pound of sugar, a large pint of yeast. Strew your seeds and sugar in the flour then rub in the butter. Mix some new milk with the yeast and work it in your flour putting in milk still by degrees till it's wet enough. Then work it as you would bread letting it stand to rise before the fire till it is soft. Make it into flat or round rolls and so bake them. Before they are too hard split the round ones and put the long ones in long sleeves. Put them in the oven again till they are crisp and brown.

Saffron Cakes

Take a pound of flour well dried and rub in half a pound of butter and half a pound of sugar. (Take) a quarter of an ounce of saffron, dry it very well and beat it very fine then put it into half a pint of cream and boil it. When it is almost cold put in six eggs and beat the eggs and cream together with a pint of yeast. Mix this altogether in the flour and let it be like a good paste. Make it in little cakes and bake it upon tins. Set it before the fire to rise. They must be baked in a slow oven. Be sure to prick them.

The colour and flavour of these would be quite intense. Elizabeth David in *Spices, Salt and Aromatics in the English Kitchen* suggests one grain of saffron to colour and flavour a pound of rice. The quantity in this recipe is one hundred grains!

Shrewsbury Cakes

Take half a peck of fine flour, half an ounce of beaten cinnamon, six eggs, two pounds of sugar, two pounds and a half of butter and a little rosewater. Put all these together and work it well up to a paste. Roll them out and cut them in what shape you please and put them on buttered papers and bake them.

(Some earlier versions of this recipe were flavoured with ginger. John Murrell's cookery book of 1621, *A Delightful Daily Exercise for Ladies and Gentlewomen* omits the eggs and cinnamon but adds 'a nutmeg grated'. The first cinnamon flavoured Shrewsbury cakes are said to date from the 1670s).

Wiggs

Take five quarts of flour well dried, half a pound of sugar, some caraway seeds, ginger and nutmeg pounded and mixed with the flour as also the seeds, five eggs and three whites, almost three pints of ale yeast that is not bitter, a pint of good milk and a pound of unwashed butter melted in the milk. Mix it all together for a good while. It must be high and very tough. Roll them in flour and sugar in little long cakes. Put them in an oven and take them out when they heave.

Wiggs (also spelt whigs or wigs) were usually eaten at breakfast. The recipe above is a basic one: Dorothy Hartley in *Food in England* gives a variety of recipes from 1700 to 1900 which add ginger, nutmeg, candied peel and dried fruits.

> *Thou shalt eat curds and cream, all the year lasting,*
> *And drink the crystal stream, pleasant in tasting;*
> *Wig and whey till thou burst, and bramble berries;*
> *Pie-lid and pasty-crust, pears, plums and cherries.*
>
> Elizabethan ballad.

PUDDINGS & PIES

The Pudding is a Dish very difficult to be described because of the several sorts there are of it: Flour, Milk, Eggs, Sugar, Suet, Marrow, Raisins etc are the most common ingredients of it ... BLESSED BE HE THAT INVENTED PUDDING, for it is a Manna that hits the Palates of all Sorts of People ... Ah, What an excellent thing is an English Pudding. To come in Pudding Time, is as much as to say, to come in the most lucky Moments in the World.

M. Misson: *Memoirs and Observations in England* 1719

Oatmeal Pudding

Of oats decorticated take two pound
And of new milk enough the same to drown
Of raisins of the sun, ston'd, ounces eight
Of currants cleanly picked, an equal weight;
Of suet finely slic'd, an ounce at least;

And six eggs newly taken from the nest:
Season this mixture well with salt and spice;
'Twill make a pudding far exceeding rice;
And you may safely feed on it like farmers,
For the receipt is learned Dr Harmer's.

William King (1663-1712)

The manuscript includes numerous sweet dishes, many of them very close to sixteenth or seventeenth century recipes. There are syllabubs, flummeries, creams and custards as well as such elegant devices as 'A Duck's Nest' and 'A Hedgehog'. Most recipes use considerable quantities of cream, eggs and butter often combined with spices, sack or other sweet wines. A number of the recipes are similar to those which can be found in contemporary cookery books such as 'The Compleat City and Country Cook' published in 1732 and written by Charles Carter who had been employed by a number of aristocratic households.

Almond Cheese
Take a quart of new milk. Beat five eggs both yolks and whites very well and mix with the milk. Put in a nutmeg quartered, set it over the fire and let it boil quick till it turns to a firm curd and whey. Pour it into a colander and let it stand an hour. Take out the nutmeg and beat the curd in a mortar till it is tender. Sweeten it with fine sugar, orange flower water and sack. Put it again into the colander and let it stand till stiff. Turn it out and cover it with cream.

Almond Cream
Take a quarter of a pound of sweet almonds. Blanch and beat them very fine and put to them a pint of cream. Boil the almonds and cream together, put in the whites of two eggs very well beat. Set it on the fire till it just boils and grows thick then sweeten it as you like and pour it in your basin.

Almond Custard
Boil a quart of cream with cinnamon, mace, two or three cloves, ginger and nutmeg. When the cream does taste of the spice strain it out into a quarter of a pound of almonds blanched and finely beat with rosewater and eight or nine yolks of eggs. Sweeten it to your taste and bake it on a pot of water. When it is baked and cold stick it with slices of dates or suckets.

Suckets were sweets made by candying citrus peels, the stalks of plants such as angelica, green walnuts or unripened fruit. For example:

To Candy Cowslips or any Flowers or Greens
Steep gum arabic in water. Wet the flowers or greens with it. Shake them in a cloth that they may not be too wet then dip them in fine sifted sugar. Hang them on a string tied across a chimney that has a fire in. They must hang two or three days till they are dry. They are pretty in a dessert.

Apple pies seem to have endured in popularity in English cookery. In 1664 there was published *The Court and Kitchen of Elizabeth commonly called Joan Cromwell*, widow of the Lord Protector, Oliver. Her recipe 'To Make a Double Tart' begins with a filling of codling apples, sugar, cloves and cinnamon baked in a pastry crust. A custard of 'a quart of cream, six eggs, a quartern of sugar and a sliced nutmeg' was then added before a second baking of eight minutes. The final touch was to replace the original lid with 'a lid cut in flowers ... lay it on and garnish it with preserves of damsons, raspberries, apricots and cherries and place a preserved quince in the middle and strew it with sugar biskets'. The recipe casts a wholly new light on the term 'puritanical'.

A century and a half later apple pies were still a subject of interest: Jane Austen wrote to her sister, Cassandra, on October 17 1815:

'I am glad the new cook begins so well. Good apple pies are a considerable part of our domestic happiness'. However some years earlier she had confessed in another letter to be grateful for the departure of guests for 'I shall be left to the comfortable disposal of my time, to ease of mind from the torments of rice puddings and apple dumplings'.

The recipe given in the manuscript is unusual in that it uses a hot water crust and a very high proportion of butter to flour:

Apple Pie

(Take) half a pound of flour and half a pound of butter. Put your butter in a pan and pour the quantity of water you think will mix your flour boiling hot on it. When your butter is dissolved and almost cold beat up the yolks of two eggs in it then mix it into your flour and make it up pretty soft. Roll out your paste and put half at the bottom of your patty pan and save the other half for the top. Take a dozen of very good pippins, pare them and cut them crossways as you do an orange and take the core out very clean. Lay them the flat side downwards then take the peel of a lemon or two and slice it very small. Strew between every layer and sweeten it very sweet with the best sugar. When your pie is ready to lid squeeze in the juice of a very good lemon over all. So lid it up and bake it very well. This crust will do for all sorts of pies.

That the eighteenth century gardener could offer the eighteenth century cook an impressive selection of varieties of apple, witness this list taken from Weston's *Gardener's and Planter's Calendar* of 1778:

Anise Apple, Aromatic Pippin, Aromatic Russet, Codlin, Costard Apple, Courpendu, Dutch Codlin, Franche Rennet, French Pippin, Golden Pippin, Golden Rennet, Golden Russet, John Apple, Harvey Apple, Haute Bonte, Holland Pippin, Juneating, Kentish Pippin, Kentish Fill-basket, Kirton Pippin, Lady Thigh, Langton None-such, Lemon Pippin, Loan's Pearmain, Margaret Apple, Monstrous Rennet, Nonpareil Old and New, Nutmeg Apple, Partridge Apple, Pear Russet, Pile's Russet, Pomme D'Api, Quince Apple, Rambour, Red Autumn Calville, Rennette Grise, Royal Pearmain, Royal Russet, Salmon Apple, Stone Pippin, Summer Calville, Summering, Summer Pearmain, Summer Pippin, Summer Russet, Ten Shillings Apple, Violet Apple, Wheeler's Russet, White Autumn Calville, White Kentish Pippin, Winter Gilliflower, Winter Queening.

Blancmange

Take two ounces of isinglass. Steep it all night in rosewater then take it out of the water and put it into a quart of milk with six laurel leaves broken into two or three pieces each leaf. Boil this softly till the isinglass is dissolved then put to it a pint of cream and boil it till 'tis near half wasted. Strain it through a thin strainer and leave as little of the isinglass in the bag as you can. Sweeten it pretty well and let it settle a little. Put it into moulds first wet with cold water to make it turn out easy or (onto) a flat earthen or china dish until the next day. When you use it you may cut it with a jagging iron in long slips and lay it in knots on a dish or plate.

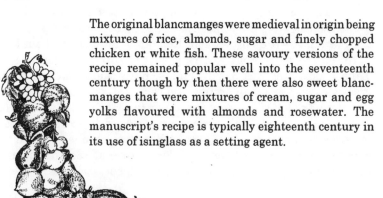

The original blancmanges were medieval in origin being mixtures of rice, almonds, sugar and finely chopped chicken or white fish. These savoury versions of the recipe remained popular well into the seventeenth century though by then there were also sweet blancmanges that were mixtures of cream, sugar and egg yolks flavoured with almonds and rosewater. The manuscript's recipe is typically eighteenth century in its use of isinglass as a setting agent.

A Boiled Rice Pudding

Take three ounces of ground rice and a pint of cream. stir it gently over a gentle fire with a blade of mace till it's so thick as the spoon will stand in it. Take six eggs leaving out half the whites very well beaten and strained and a little sack and sugar to your taste. Melt three ounces of fresh butter and when it is almost cold stir it together. Butter the china basin you boil it in very well and be sure it is full when you tie the cloth on or you will spoil it. Three quarters of an hour boils it.

Burnt Cream

A pint of cream, the yolks of eight eggs and a spoonful of flour: beat it well together and make it pretty sweet. Put in a bay leaf and some lemon peel cut thin. Boil it till it is very thick keeping it stirring very well for fear it should burn. Put it into your side dish and scrape some fine sugar over it. Brown it well with a hot salamander (a metal implement heated over coals until red hot and then held over a dish to 'grill' it). Send it up hot.

Caramel with China Oranges

Take four China oranges, peel and split them into quarters. Take care you do not break them for if any wet comes out they will not do. Lay the quarters before the fire on tins to dry, turn them and dry the skins till they are tough. Take half a pound of fine sugar sifted through a hair sieve, put it in a silver or brass pan, set it over a slow fire without water, stirring it till it is melted and looks clear. Then take it off the fire and put in your orange quarters one at a time. Take them out as fast as you can with a teaspoon and lay them on a buttered earthen dish or they will stick. The sugar will keep hot enough to do any plate full.

N.B. Any fruit in summer may be done the same way, or roasted chestnuts. Observe they must be done just before you use them for they will not keep.

The manuscript's numerous recipes for orange pastes, creams, drops, buttered oranges and orange butter as well as orange wines, marmalade and preserved oranges show the popularity of the fruit. Although this recipe is the only one which specifies China oranges Jane Grigson in her 'Fruit Book' explains that in older recipes 'sometimes you will see that

Portugal or China oranges are called for and that is the sweet kind – but up until the early nineteenth century it is safe to conclude that the word orange means what we call a Seville or marmalade orange'. Although there had been imports of citrus fruits since the Middle Ages it was not until the seventeenth century that China oranges reached this country via Portugal. In 1666 Samuel Pepys had helped himself to his first orange from a tree in Lord Brooke's garden. Three years later he was still a little cautious:

1669 March 9 ... to my cousin Stradwicks ... and here met my cousin Roger, and his wife and my cousin Turner; and here, which I never did before, I drank a glass, of a pint I believe, at one draught, of the juice of oranges of whose peel they make comfits; and here they drink the juice as wine, with sugar, and it is a very fine drink; but it being new, I was doubtful whether it might not do me hurt.

> *Here oranges sweet*
> *From China they come*
> *Here apples and pears*
> *And sweet orline plum.*

Nineteenth century street cry

Chocolate Cream
Take a quarter of a pound of chocolate, break it into a quarter of a pint of water. Mill it and boil it with a little sugar till the chocolate is melted then put to it a pint of cream and two eggs well beat. Let it boil milling it all the while it does boil. When it is cold mill it again that it may go up in the basin with a great froth.

Churned Syllabub
Take a quart of cream. Churn it till it's thick but not to turn it then take a pint of sack or sweet white wine with the pieces of one lemon and a little lemon peel with some sugar and nutmeg to your taste. Pour your cream to it and stir it together, put it in glasses and let it stand all night.

Citron Cream
Take half a pound of citron, cut it as thin as possibly you can and in pieces about half an inch long. Put it into a large pint of cream with a piece of lemon rind cut very thin. Boil it a quarter of an hour

then take it off and put in the yolk of an egg well beaten. Set it on the fire again till it grows thick then take it off the fire and put in the juice of a lemon by degrees keeping it stirring till it is quite cold.

Clotted Cream

Take four gallons of milk. Let it just boil up then pour in two quarts of cream and when it begins to boil again put it into large flat pans or trays. Let it stand three days then take it off from the milk with a skimmer full of holes. Lay it on a china dish laying it high in the middle. Eat it with milk, sugar or wine.

The manuscript describes this as 'clouted' cream, the spelling and usage common until the middle of the eighteenth century. In 1698 Celia Fiennes, travelling through the West Country, visited St. Austell:

My landlady brought me one of the West Country tarts, this was the first I had met with, though I had asked for them in many places in Somerset and Devonshire. It's an apple pie with a custard all on the top, it's the most acceptable entertainment that could be made me; they scald their cream and milk in most parts of those countries and so it's a sort of clouted cream as we call it, with a little sugar and so put on top of the apple pie; I was much pleased with my supper though not with the custom of the country, which is a universal smoking. Both men, women and children have all their pipes of tobacco in their mouths and so sit round the fire smoking.

A century later the Cornish writer Richard Polwhele noted the popularity of 'clouted' cream describing it as 'poured profusely' on 'the squab pie, the herb pie (and) the leek and pork pie.

Cream Flummery

Take a pint of sweet cream, three spoonfuls of rice flour very finely sifted, then beat two ounces of blanched almonds with a little milk to keep them from oiling. The whites of three eggs beat very well, put to the cream and strain them on the almonds. Set it on the fire and stir it all one way till it's thick and smooth as a custard then pour it into cups or glasses. When you use it turn it out upon a china plate.

Earlier flummeries were thickened with oatmeal: this version is very much a late seventeenth century recipe. Elizabeth Raffald in *The Expe-*

*rienced English Housekeeper, for the Use and Ease of Ladies, House-
keepers, Cooks etc. Wrote Purely from Practice* published in 1769, sets a
sweetened mixture of pounded almonds and cream with 'a pint of calf's
foot stock'. Later still flummeries were set in elaborately shaped moulds
frequently flavoured with fruit and coloured with a variety of dyes.

A Good Green

Lay an ounce of Gamboge in half a quarter of a pint of water till
it is melted then take an ounce and a half of stone blue dissolved
in a little water. When melted put it to a quarter of a pound of fine
sugar and a quarter of a pint of water more and let it boil. Put in
a spoonful of this to a pint of white clear cakes and it will make
them a very good green.

Other Colours

For red Carmine, for blue Smalt, for green powder called Green
Earth, for yellow Saffron, (for) brown Chocolate.

Cream Tart

Take a quart of cream and boil it. Beat eight eggs and and put to
it but have a care it does not curdle. Sweeten it very well and grate
in a nutmeg. Take the marrow of two bones, cut it small and put
in with it half a pound of currants picked and washed and a good
handful of spinach well picked and washed and likewise cut small.
Roll a sheet of paste and lay on the bottom of your dish. Cross bars
of paste on the top with sugar.

Custards

A pint of cream: boil it with a blade or two of mace and half a
nutmeg. Let it stand to be cold close covered or stirring so to
prevent skinning over. (Take) the yolks of six and the whites of
three eggs very well beat with rose or orange flower water and well
sweetened. Strain your eggs into the cream and bake them in
china cups.

Another cream-based custard recipe is spiced with a blade of mace and
'twenty corns Jamaica pepper' and a third is wine-based.

Dutch Custards

A pint of white wine and half a pound of fine sugar.
Boil it and let it stand to be cold then take six eggs both yolks and
whites. Beat them very well then mix them with the wine. Put in
the juice of two large lemons then put it into a silver or china basin
and set it on a very slow fire to bake. Set it to cool and just before
you send it up rasp the rind of a clear lemon lightly over it.

A Duck's Nest

Make a pretty stiff hartshorn or calves' foot jelly. Run it off fine as
for glasses. Put it while hot into a glass bowl that has a cover. Fill
it about half full. Let it stand till next day that it may be perfectly
cold. In the meantime blow six or eight eggs, take the shells and
stop the least hole with a bit of putty. Fill them with water or
rather let them lie full of water some time before you stop the hole.
Shake out the water and set them upright in a dish of salt. Fill
them whilst wet with either blancmange or hartshorn flummery
(if blancmange let it first settle well and not be too stiff). You must
keep filling them as they shrink down till quite full and cold.
For a penny you may buy a doll's tin funnel fit for this purpose.
Pare some lemon peel thin, long and without any white. Let it lie
in fair water till you have time with a pair of scissors to cut it in
narrow slips like straw. Strew some of these over your jelly in the
glass, then take your eggs and just dip them in warm water and
with care break and take off the shell. Lay them on the straw in
the bowl and strew some more of the lemon peel over them and put
on your glass cover. If some of the lemon peel hangs out it looks
more natural. If you have no glass bowl a china bowl will do.

Fine Colours for Creams and Jellies

Red: take half an ounce of cochineal, a quarter
of an ounce of cream of tartar, a quarter of an
ounce of rock alum. Boil these in a quart of
spring water to a pint. Strain it through a jelly
bag and set it by for use. Put a spoonful or two
into any cream or jelly.

Blue: take a pint of lemon juice and two quarts of violets close tied down in a pot or jar. Set it in a pot of water to infuse. When it is infused strain it off clear. Take a pound and a quarter of sugar to a pint of this liquor and let it just boil to a syrup. Skim it well and let it stand to be cold then bottle it. It will keep for years if kept in a cold place.

A Fine Oatmeal Pudding

The yolks of eight and the whites of four eggs very well beat with some nutmeg. Put in a pint of cream and a large handful of marrow, a quarter of a pound of candied citron and orange cut thin, sugar to your taste and a large handful of oatmeal beat and sifted very fine. Stir it well together. Butter your dish. It will take an hour baking or boiling.

Gooseberry Tansy

Put a quart of gooseberries into a frying pan with a little butter, mash and fry them until they are soft. Beat seven yolks and four whites of eggs with two spoonfuls of sack. Grate the crumb of a stale penny loaf very fine and sugar to your taste. Put these to the gooseberries and stir them well together, then fry it in a clean pan with good butter. When you send it up strew on sugar.

The original 'tansy' was a medieval relative of the omelette, taking its name from the tansy juice used to flavour a fried mixture of other herbs and beaten eggs. The recipe developed with the addition of breadcrumbs, cream, spices and eventually, as in the version above, fruit.

A Hedgehog

Take a pint of sweet and a pint of sour cream with a blade of mace and a piece of nutmeg. Let it boil. Beat six yolks of eggs and stir it both ways to curdle then run it through a cloth to whey and hang it up. When it is dry mix in half a pound of sweet almonds well beat with some fine sugar. Make it up in the shape of a hedgehog. Stick currants for the eyes and mouth, and stick the back with slit almonds. Put it in a dish with whipped cream about it.

Ice Cream

Take tin ice pots. Fill them with cream either sweetened or plain or fruit in it. Shut your pots very close. To six pots you must allow twenty pounds of ice. Breaking some of the ice in very small pieces you must lay some great pieces at the bottom and top. Then take a pail and lay some straw at the bottom and put in some large pieces of ice. Put in amongst it a pound of bay salt, set in the pots and lay ice salt between every pot that they may not touch one another. The ice must lie round them on every side. Lay a good deal of ice on the top. Cover the pail with straw, set it in a cellar where no sun or light comes in. It will be frozen in four hours but it may stand longer. Take it out just before you use it, hold it in the pots in your hands and it will slip out. When you would freeze any sort of fruit either cherries, strawberries, currants or raspberries put them into lemonade made with spring water and lemon juice sweetened. Put enough in the pots to make the fruit hang together and put them into the ice as you did the cream.

The preservative effects of ice were well known to the eighteenth century cook; ice-houses had long been constructed to use the principle of insulation to keep winter ice for domestic use. A century earlier Pepys recounts how ' ... fowl killed in December Alderman Barker said he did buy, and putting into the box under his sledge, did forget to take them out to eat till April next, and they then were found there, and were through the frost as sweet and fresh and eat as well as at first killed'.

By the early eighteenth century five hundred thousand tons of ice were being imported annually from Scandinavia and even America. William Cobbett in the ninth pamphlet of his series on *Cottage Economy* published in 1821-2 gives detailed instructions for the construction and maintenance of an ice-house though he confesses that 'not caring enough about fresh meat and fish in summer' he has not used the instructions himself and that 'there is however in all cases this comfort, that if the thing fail as an ice-house, it will serve all generations to come as a model for a pig-bed'!

Those who managed to keep their ice-houses pig-free could use this recipe which, as an unbeaten mixture of cream and fruit, is clearly an early example. By the end of the eighteenth century much more sophisticated recipes were in use giving instructions to remove and beat the mixture half way through the freezing process in order to improve the texture.

Lemon Cream

Take a pint and a half of water and rasp in the rinds of three clear lemons, cover it and let it stand an hour then squeeze in the juice of six lemons. Beat the whites of six fresh eggs but not to a froth, put them into the lemon water and strain it through a hair sieve. Sweeten it to taste. Set it on the fire in a flat saucepan and keep it stirring till it's thick. If you let it have one boil it will not hurt it. Put it into jelly glasses.

Lemon Pudding

The crumb of a white penny loaf, six yolks and three whites of eggs very well beat. Put to it the juice of six lemons and the outermost rind of them rasped in after they are well stirred and mixed together with half a pound of fine sugar. When you put it into the oven melt half a pound of butter and pour all over the pudding. Make a little roll of paste and put round your dish to keep the pudding in. Half an hour will bake it.

Lemon or Orange Pudding

Take the rinds of two oranges or lemons and boil them in two waters till the bitterness is out. Pound them in a mortar with the juice and meat till it is very fine. Grate three biscuits and put to it half a pound of melted butter, the yolk of six eggs, a little sack, half a pint of cream, half a candied orange, as much lemon and as much citron cut in thin slices. Grate in a nutmeg. Mix all well together, put puff paste at the bottom of your dish. Not a rash oven.

Marrow Pudding

Take a pint of cream. Scald it with a blade of mace and half a nutmeg. Let it stand till cold then put to it the yolks of six and whites of three eggs well beaten with rose or orange flower water. Sweeten it pretty sweet. Strain the eggs into the cream. Lay a thin puff paste in your dish, then some very thin slices of white bread, thirty raisins stoned and plumped, or currants plumped, citron, orange and lemon peel candied, cut thin in slices and the marrow of at least a very good bone in pretty thick lumps. Last of all pour on your custard. A little above half an hour will bake it.

New College Puddings

Take half a pound of beef suet cut very small, a quarter of a pound of currants, half a pound of Naples Biscuits, the yolks of six eggs and one white, a little cream or rosewater, some salt, nutmeg and allspice, three ounces of sweetmeats. Roll it into six balls then take half a pound of good butter, put it into a frying pan, make it hot then put in your puddings. Cover them close and turn them with care. Sack and melted butter for sauce.

Orange Butter

Take the rinds of two or three oranges, boil them very tender then beat them in a marble mortar and rub them through a hair sieve. Take a quart of good cream, boil it and put the yolks of ten eggs and the whites of two very well beat before mixed with the cream. Stir it all one way till it is a curd. Put it into a clean sieve when it is cold and let the whey run from it. Mix in as much of your orange as will make it taste to your liking. When it's sweetened put it on a china plate.

Orange Puddings

Pare, as for preserving, six Seville oranges. Cut out a small piece at one end and scoop out all the meat then boil them very tender in shifted waters. When drained scoop out the rest of the loose pulp and have your pudding ready made with the meat you scooped out of the oranges, the yolks of six eggs, half a pound of butter, two or three Naples biscuits with sugar and orange flower water to your taste. Let these ingredients be beat very fine in a marble mortar and rubbed through a hair sieve. So fill your oranges and put the pieces on again then put them in an earthen pan that will just hold them and keep one another upright for they must not stand one upon another. Put into your pan as much sugar and water as will almost cover them but it must not go into them. Cover them with a plate and bake them in an oven fit for a tansy. When baked shake them out and drain away the syrup. Sack and butter for the sauce. You may make them of China oranges but must rub them of salt to take out the bitterness instead of paring them.

A Paplin

Take cheese curd, eight eggs, the whites of four, a quarter of a pound of butter and as much sugar. First break the curd very well then mix it all well together. Take a sheet of white paper, rub it well with butter and put the stuff upon it. Set it in a moderate oven – half an hour will bake it – and when you take it out of the oven cut off the top. Slice citron upon it, pour upon that butter, sugar and a little orange-flower water. Lay the top on again and serve it up.

(Not even the *Shorter Oxford Dictionary* can offer any definition or history of the name of this particular dish).

Pistachio Cream

Take half a pound of pistachio nuts. Break, blanch and beat the kernels all except a dozen which you must keep to lay on top of your cream when you send it up. Beat the kernels with a little milk then put them into a pint of cream with the yolks of two eggs well beaten, some fine sugar and a spoonful of the juice of spinach. Set it over the fire and let it just boil then put it into your basin or glasses. When it is cold slice your kernels and lay them on the top of your cream.

Rhenish Cream or Blancmange

About two ounces of isinglass boiled in water, a stick of cinnamon, five or six cloves and some mace with some preserved apricots, near a bottle of Rhenish or Lisbon wine, a piece of lemon peel, juice of three oranges and the same of lemon or to taste with a piece of orange peel and sugar to taste. Boil all together. Observe to put in lastly the yolks of eight or nine eggs well beat and not boil it afterwards but bruise them well together and just scald in the eggs.

Spanish Butter

Take two gallons of milk. Boil it and whilst boiling put in a quart of cream. Let it boil after the cream is in then set it in two broad pans. Let it stand two or three days then take the cream from the milk into a silver dish or wooden bowl. Put to it a spoonful of orange flower water with a perfumed pastille or two melted in. Sweeten it a little with sifted sugar then beat it all one way with a silver ladle till it's stiff enough to lie as high as you would have it.

A Thick Raw Cream

Take two trays and keep them boiling hot and when you bring home your milk put it into the scalding hot tray and cover it with the other hot tray. The next day you will find a thick cream. This must be done the day before you use it.

A Trifle

Take a pint of cream and one spoonful of orange-flower water. Sweeten and boil it. Put it in the basin you send it up in. When almost cold put in a spoonful of rennet and let it stand till it comes like cheese.

This recipe is a clear descendant of the trifles of the sixteenth and seventeenth centuries which consisted of warmed cream sweetened and flavoured with spices and pre-dates the eighteenth century recipes which added layers of custard and sponge biscuits soaked in sack. The name meant, quite literally 'a trifle' i.e. something small, of no importance. Although the trifle has survived, much altered, into the twentieth century, its close cousin, the 'whim-wham' has not!

DRINKS

The Raisin Wine and Brandy Warehouse, in Catherine Street, in the Strand.
Brandy at four shillings per gallon, brought to such perfection by a New Method of Making, that is difficult to be distinguished from Foreign ...

The Whitehall Evening Post or, London Intelligencer
August 21-24 1756

Sunday, Feb. 8, 1754 - ... if I am at home, or in company abroad, I will never drink more than four glasses of strong beer: one to toast the King's health, the second to the Royal Family, the third to all friends, and the fourth to the pleasure of the company. If there is either wine or punch, never upon any terms or persuasion to drink more than eight glasses, each glass to hold no more than a half a quarter of a pint.

Thomas Turner
The Diary of a Georgian Shopkeeper

Tea, coffee and chocolate were all well known and widely available, though expensive, drinks by the mid-eighteenth century. The manuscript makes no mention of coffee and only passing reference to tea. Chocolate is included but only as an ingredient in three recipes – for Chocolate Almonds, Chocolate Puffs and Chocolate Cream. Many recipes include a variety of wines and spirits: sack and 'Rhenish wine', rum, geneva [gin] and brandy. Though some of the wine recipes use added yeasts others use the far older process of natural fermentation.

Barley Water

You must just boil a little barley in some water then pour the water out and fill up the mug with fresh boiling water. Let it stand on the barley two or three hours and then pour it clear off. When you put on the fresh water put some lemon peel in which gives it a pretty taste and colour.

Barley water had long been known as a drink suitable for invalids: earlier versions were flavoured with a variety of herbs or with licorice. Flavouring with lemon was a seventeenth century development.

Cowslip Wine

Take eight gallons of water and twenty pounds of loaf sugar. Boil it for one hour and skim it till it be very clear. When it is blood warm pour it into a vessel filled with two bushels of picked cowslips and put twelve or fourteen spoonfuls of new ale yeast. Cover it till next day then squeeze in the juice of sixteen large lemons and the peel of eight. Stir it very frequently for four days then stop it close and let it stand then bottle it off. It will keep two or three years.

Elder Wine

Take Malaga raisins, pick the great stalks from them and chop them. Put to every twenty pounds of fruit five gallons of water which must be first boiled and stood till it be little more than blood warm. Stir them well together, cover them and let it stand and work twelve or fourteen days stirring them twice a day. Before they stood their time have a quantity of elder berries full but not rotten ripe picked from the stalks. Bruise and boil them then strain them. To every five gallons of liquor strained from the raisins put six pints of clear elder juice. Put it into a wine vessel. Lay the bung lightly over the hole and do not stop it as long as it makes the least singing in the barrel. Sometimes it will work six weeks. When it has done stop it close and so let it stand in a warm place three months.

Milk Punch

Take the peel of fifteen lemons, very thin, infused in a pint and a half of brandy forty-eight hours, two pounds of double refined sugar dissolved in three quarts of water, the juice of the fifteen lemons, three quarts of brandy besides that the peel was infused in, three pints of milk with one grated nutmeg made scalding hot and poured into the above.

Let it all stand together twelve hours then strain it through a flannel bag until fine.

Another

In four quarts of water steep the rinds of eighteen lemons cut small, for the space of forty-eight hours in an earthen pan. Add five quarts of spring water and near two pounds of loaf sugar. Stir it till all the sugar is dissolved. Cut the eighteen lemons in halves and scoop out the insides. Two quarts of milk scalding hot but take care it does not boil. Keep it stirring till it become whey, put in the other ingredients, grate in a nutmeg and cover all with a cloth. Let it stand an hour then pour it into a large jelly bag and let it run quite clear as rock water. It may be boiled directly. It will keep a twelve month.

Milk punches became fashionable early in the eighteenth century: some of the recipes are similar to those for the possets which were often given to invalids as a substitute for a meal. Elizabeth Raffald in *The Experienced English Housekeeper* published in 1782 gives a recipe for a wine posset that uses 'the crumb of a penny loaf' to thicken a mixture of milk, wine, and sugar flavoured with nutmeg. Richer kinds of posset, served in special posset dishes or posset pots, were served at formal meals.

Orange Posset

Squeeze the juice of two seville oranges and one lemon into a china basin that holds about a quart. Sweeten it like syrup with double refined sugar. Put to it half a spoonful of orange flower water then strain it through a sieve. Boil a large pint of cream with some of the orange peel cut thin. When it is pretty cold run it through a flannel bag into the juices. You must hold the bag as high as you can from the basin. It must stand a day before you use it.

Orange Wine

Pare very thin and squeeze the juice over the peels of one hundred fine seville oranges. Boil for half an hour fourteen gallons of water. Let it stand till milk-warm then pour it over the juice and peels and so let it stand twenty-four hours. Then take twentyfive pounds of lisbon sugar and stir it in. Take twelve lemons and peel them. Make syrup of them and put to your orange wine with four quarts of Rhenish wine. Strain it all into a barrel and lay a paper over the bunghole for a week and then stop it up. Put a peg at the top to give it vent now and then. Let it stand three or four months then bottle it.

As excise duties made imported wines and spirits more expensive home-made raisin wines were suggested as a cheaper alternative. Ronald Fletcher in *The Parkers at Saltram 1769-89* gives the prices of some imports '... You could buy a bottle of Superior Old Port for three shillings, Prime Old Sherry for three shillings and sixpence, Prime Madeira for five shillings. You could have a gallon of Cognac Brandy for twenty shillings, of Old Jamaica Rum for fifteen shillings and Hollands Geneva Gin for ten shillings'.

Raisin Wine

Put five pounds of Smyrna raisins neither picked nor stalked to a gallon of cold water. Fill the cask alternately with raisins and water till it is within a gallon of being full, if the cask contains nine gallons. Take three ounces of hops and boil them in two quarts with which when cold fill up the cask with hops and all. Put a brown paper over the bung hole and in about three weeks you'll go near to find it sufficiently fermented. Put into nine gallons two quarts of brandy then bung it down. In about eight months it will be fit to drink.

Sack Posset

Take nine eggs with four whites. Beat them with half a pint of sack or half a pint of good beer and some powdered sugar – if beer six spoonfuls and if sack four spoonfuls. When well beaten together stir it over the fire till it be very thick but not curdled. Then take a pint of cream or three pints of new milk before boiled and something cooled. So pour it into the eggs with great force till it froths. Cover it close for a quarter of an hour. Strew sugar round it before you serve it up.

To Make Salop Jelly

To a pint of boiling water put a quarter of an ounce of the powder of salop and let it boil for a quarter of an hour or thereabouts till you think the jelly strong enough with a little stick of cinnamon a little bruised and about half a lemon peel. Take it from the fire and squeeze in the juice of one lemon and run it through a jelly bag. Put to it half a pint of rhenish wine and set it on the fire again but not to boil. Sweeten it to your taste with double refined sugar and send it up hot.

N.B. Salop is the ground dried root of *orchis mascula*. It was in common use as an ingredient in both hot and cold drinks throughout the eighteenth and nineteenth centuries. Dorothy Hartley in *Food in England* describes how 'in Scotland I had it laced with spirits in a glass. In Ireland it was served in a teacup thickened with cream and egg yolk'.

Shrub

Take three quarts of rum, a quart of the juice of Seville orange and the juice of one lemon, one pound of double refined sugar. Strain out all the seeds and pare all your oranges before you squeeze them. To a five gallon cask put the peels of four oranges, let it stand till it's fine which will be in about six weeks then bottle it.
N.B. as much rum as juice will keep it two years.

Shrub is still made commercially: rumour has it that it originated in Cornwall, made by thrifty Cornish smugglers when their cargoes of rum were tainted by salt water

White Elder Wine

Chop six pounds of raisins very small. Put to them one gallon of water and let them infuse ten days. Stir them twice a day then put in half a peck of elderflowers. Put the juice likewise of six lemons, infuse the flowers three or four days then strain it off.

Doubtless though Cobbett believed the best drink to be home brewed beer he would also have found the above recipes acceptable. Certainly he would have preferred them to tea which he detested: ' ... it is notorious that tea has no useful strength in it; that it contains nothing nutritious; that it besides being good for nothing, has badness in it, because it is well known to produce lack of sleep in many cases, to shake and weaken the nerves.'

COSMETICS & DOMESTICS

Now you expect some account of our cousin Spencer. They were married on Thursday between eight and nine at night ... her clothes were white satin embroidered with silver, very fine lace ... the rest of her clothes are a pink and silver, a flowered silk, white ground, a blue damask night-gown [evening dress] and a white damask the robing and facings embroidered with gold and colours, a plain pink poudesoy [peau de soie], a flowered silk, green ground, her laces and linen very fine ...

The Wedding of Georgiana Carteret - 1734
Described by Mary Delany

My dear Catherine ... do take this pin out of my sleeve. I am afraid it has torn a hole already. I shall be quite sorry if it has, for this is a favourite gown, though it cost but nine shillings a yard.

Jane Austen: *Northanger Abbey*

Though most country towns in the eighteenth century had a range of shops it was not possible to buy ready made clothes. When Jane Austen, in letters and novels, discusses the purchase of a 'gown' she was in fact describing the purchase of a dress length of material which could then be made up by the local dressmaker. By the end of the century over a dozen women's magazines existed: some were devoted to detailed illustrations of the latest fashions. One of these periodicals 'The Fashions of London and Paris' was said to be 'of the highest utility to milliners, dressmakers and private families in the country and in all parts of Europe'. In the country fabrics and haberdashery might be bought from travelling drapers or the 'lacemen' who travelled from village to village.

The manuscript has a variety of instructions for dying and laundering fabrics and lace as well as for making such useful commodities as ink, soap and simple cosmetics. Maggie Angeloglou in 'A History of Make-up'

87

describes the dangers of eighteenth century cosmetics: since the six-teenth century fashionable young ladies had lost their hair and, in more extreme cases, their lives from the poisonous qualities of the white lead used to give them a fashionably pale complexion. Mercury was often an ingredient of 'face washes' intended to improve complexions damaged by smallpox and if these failed ' ... dung, minced veal and goat hair were ... allayed with lemon juice, milk or cucumber water'.

Face Water
Of the two cosmetic versions of 'face water' one contains veal, raisins, lemons, yet another pint of snails, bitter almonds, brandy, white wine and elderflowers, the whole to be 'put in a limbeck and still (i.e. distilled) with a slow fire'. A more acceptable version 'To Wash the Face and Neck' is this:

A pound and a half of pearl barley makes twelve quarts of water, a pound and a half of bitter almonds pounded very fine, one quart of fine old rum, one ounce and a half of camphor put an equal bit in each bottle then stop it up close for use.

The Pomatum for the Hands
About a dram of white wax, two drams of spermaceti [a white wax-like substance obtained from the sperm-whale], one ounce of oil of bitter almonds. Slice your wax very thin, put it in a basin over boiling water. When it is melted put in the spermaceti. Stir it together then put in the oil. When all is melted stir it up with a bone knife till cold, then beat it up in rosewater till it is white. Keep it in water and change the water once a day.

This is certainly preferable to another eighteenth-century 'Hand Poma-tum' which used an ounce of 'sweet essence' in a mixture of washed beef suet, mutton fat and wax.

Paste to Wash Hands
Take a pound of bitter almonds, blanch and beat them very fine in a mortar with four ounces of figs. When it comes to a paste put it in a gallipot and keep it for use. A little at a time will serve.

Lip Salve

Pomatum three ounces, white wax one ounce, spermaceti one dram, double refined sugar two ounces, twenty raisins stoned, one pippin sliced. Put all these into a saucepan and when they are boiled enough colour at discretion with alkanet root. Put in a little Hungary water. Strain through muslin into little cakes.

Liquid Soap

Put a pound of soft soap over a gentle fire, when it begins to dissolve by degrees put in a pint of spirits of wine. When it is a little cooled put in half an ounce of white spirit of lavender and half an ounce of camphor. Let it settle and when cold bottle it.

To Clean Blond Lace

Take your lace and put it (not more than four double) into old cloth and run it slightly at each edge and in the middle to keep it quite smooth then lay it all night in sweet oil. The next day put it into a clean lather and boil it up for a quarter of an hour then squeeze it out and put it into another clean lather and boil it a quarter of an hour more, then dip it into a thin starch and squeeze it out, then take it out of the rag as much as you can iron at a time and iron it between writing paper.

To Dye Gloves Purple

Half an ounce of logwood, a quarter of an ounce of alum in a quart of water to be boiled till it comes to a pint.

To Make Dyes

Logwood and copperas for black.
Logwood and alum for purple.
Turmeric and alum for yellow. To make them stiff, gum.

A slightly more detailed set of instructions 'to dye linens yellow' explains that you must 'put your gown in dry and let it boil. Rinse it with pump water and let it stand in pump water and about a quarter of a pint of vinegar'.

To Make Ink

Take four ounces of galls, bruise them and put them to steep in a quart of rainwater for four days. Strain them out and put in two ounces of green copperas and one ounce of gum arabic. Keep it in a warm place for a fortnight shaking it well every day.

To Make Searcloth

Take a pint of sweet oil, two ounces of beeswax, two ounces of white and six ounces of red lead. Put the wax to melt in the oil and stir it well, then take both the leads and pound them well in a brass mortar. When done put them in and let them boil till they be well incorporated so that it will not stick to the knife or fingers then dip in your cloth.

In the seventeenth century searcloth had been used to make gloves to protect the hands and keep them fashionably white:

> ... searcloth gloves doth show
> To make their hand as white as snow.

Michael Drayton: *The Muses' Elysium,* 1630

To Scour Pewter

Take a bushel of the best wood ashes, put them into an ash cloth and pour in three pails of water to filter through the ashes for a day still putting up the same water to filter again until its very smooth and slippery as soap. Boil it well and when boiled near enough put in three pieces of unslaked lime about the bigness of your fist. Just let it boil after the lime is in. Let it stand to be cold then bottle it for use. Scour with fine sifted sand. Warm the lye when you use it. A little does.

The woollens which were the basic fabrics for domestic furnishings as well as for everyday clothing at the beginning of the eighteenth century were gradually replaced by other materials. G.M. Trevelyan in his *Illustrated Social History* quotes a pamphlet of 1782:

As for the ladies, they wear scarcely anything now but cotton, calicoes, muslin or silks, and think no more of woollen stuffs than we think of an old almanac. We have scarcely any woollens now about our beds but bodies warm without them.

To Wash Chintz, Printed Linen or Checked

To a handful of bran a gallon of boiling water poured over it. Strain it off the next day. Wash your linen in it warm. Repeat this if you see it necessary. Chintz and printed linens are rinsed in spring water which the oftener done the whiter they will be. Put them into water starch with a little blue in it. Hang them in the shade to dry. .

CURES & REMEDIES

The practice of physic is jostled by quacks on the one side, and by science on the other.

Peter Mere Latham 1789-1875
Collected Works, Book 1, Ch.25

We should always presume the disease to be curable, until its own nature prove it otherwise.

ibid. Ch.174

A few days since a young man, in the neighbourhood of Bath, who had been bit by a mad dog, was conveyed to Pill, to be dipped in the sea, after strong instances of the hydrophobia had appeared. In a lucid interval before he reached Pill he declared his certainty of not being able to survive the dipping, and actually died immediately after he was put into the boat.

The British Chronicle, October 24 1771

A little more than one-third of the manuscript consists of cures and remedies for a variety of ailments from the minor – nosebleeds, sore throats and corns – to the almost invariably fatal rabies, smallpox and the Plague. Eric Quayle in *Old Cook Books* explains that into the eighteenth century there 'lingered the tradition that the cook was primarily responsible for the health and general hygiene of the home and most cookery books of the period contained hints for the warding off and treatment of a variety of ills and diseases'.

Many of the remedies are optimistically labelled: there is an 'infallible' cure for rabies, salves which 'if used in time will prevent a cancer' and the following:

An Excellent Medicine against Plague

Three pints of Muscadine wine, boil in it a handful of sage and as
much rue till a pint is wasted then skim it off and set it on the fire
again and put therein of long pepper, ginger and nutmegs of each
the one third of an ounce. Beat altogether into a fine powder and
let it boil a little then put therein two ounces of treacle, one ounce
of metridate and a quarter of a pint of Angelica water. Dissolve
your treacle and metridate in the angelica water before you put
them in. Take of it both morning and evening to prevent the
infection. Keep this as your life above all worldly treasure. In the
Plague time under God trust to this for there was never man,
woman or child that it deceived. This is good also in the small-pox,
measles, surfeit or fever. It was had from a person who lived in the
City when it was infected by the Plague in 1664. Not one that took
it if infected died, nor anyone that took it by way of prevention ever
had it.

Extracted from the *London Journal*, 22 July 1721

Defoe in his *Journal of the Plague Year* lists some of the advertisements
to be seen in London:

INFALLIBLE preventive Pills against the Plague. NEVER-FAILING
Preservatives against the Infection. SOVEREIGN Cordials against the
Corruption of the Air. EXACT Regulations for the Conduct of the Body,
in case of an Infection. Antipestilential Pills. INCOMPARABLE Drink
against the Plague, never found out before. An UNIVERSAL Remedy for
the Plague. The ONLY TRUE Plague-Water. The ROYAL ANTIDOTE
against all Kinds of Infection; and such a number more that I cannot
reckon up; and if I could would fill a book themselves ...

Though outbreaks of Plague were relatively rare by the mid-eighteenth
century fear of the disease remained. The 'Bayliffe and Burgesses' of
Chippenham had, in the previous century, enacted by-laws to protect the
town from 'the infectious disease of the Plague and Pestilence'. The
Borough Minutes for 1636 record that:

Forasmuch as Henry Webb, an inhabitant Householder within the said
borough, out of his evil disposition, did of late secretly bring and procure
to be harboured within the said Borough one Arthur Estmeade, an
Inhabitant of the Town of Calne, where the plague of Pestilence is now

reigning in a most fearful manner, to the endangering of the said Inhabitants of the said Borough to be infected of the said disease by the said Arthur Estmeade (from which God defend). And thereupon the said Henry Webb being found to be a person of evil behaviour, not regarding the commonweal and tranquillity of the said borough, he the said Henry Webb is therefore upon the said thirteenth day of June ... debarred from taking any benefit at all out of the said Borough Lands until upon his submission he shall be received in again.

On the marriage of Ambrose Awdry to Christiana Delmé in 1761 he was given extensive property in Seend by his father: the property linked to the Lordship of the Manor of Seend Row included the Manor House with a range of other properties including two farms and five hundred acres of land. Ambrose Awdry later became Chapel Warden of the Vestry, an organisation which had its origins in the Church but which by the eighteenth century had assumed a wide range of local government and charitable responsibilities. He was to keep this post until 1781 and his signature can be found on the minutes of the Vestry meeting held on March 5 1780 at which it was decided '... and we do hereby further order that no overseer of the poor of the aforesaid Chapelry shall at any time or times in the continuance of such office pay or disburse any sum or sums of money to any person or persons whatsoever on any account whatsoever except on cause of pestilential disease, plague or smallpox.'

Plague may well have ceased to be a major cause of death as shown in Bills of Mortality or parish records but it clearly remained a cause for concern.

Aquemariblous

Take one ounce of the choicest cinnamon, citron rind and nutmegs of each six drams, clove, mace, cardamoms and ginger of each two drams. Bruise these altogether and macerate them twenty-four hours in juice of balm and lavender of each half a pint. Distil according to art with a moderate fire. This water is excellent to help and fortify all the noble parts of nature and, more particularly, the memory.

Bleeding at Nose

Pomegranate rind, alum, vitriol of each equal quantities. Reduce them to an extreme fine powder to be taken up the nose as snuff or put pledgets first moistened in forge water and rolled in the powder up the nostrils.

A Cure for Whooping Cough

Half an ounce of oil of amber, half an ounce of spirit of hartshorn mixed together and shook in a bottle. Rub the palms of their hands, the pit of the stomach and the soles of the feet every night and morning. Give the child a little rhubarb two or three times.

Another:

Oil of nutmeg dropt on cotton in a bag and put on the child's stomach. Palsy drops are likewise good.

Another said never to fail:

Two ounces of currants, a handful of plantain, a handful of ground ivy, a handful of five-leaf grass, boiled in three pints of spring water till one third is consumed. So drink of it as other drink.

Other 'cures' suggested included 'let the patient be blooded, vomited and given two or three gentle purges'. Suggested purges include a mixture of powdered Peruvian Bark mixed with Plague Water (q.v.), Sal Volatile, Tincture of Castor, liquid Laudanum and 'Syrup of Poppyheads'. The cure for a 'Tickling Cough' included Venice Treacle in a mixture to be taken 'the size of a horse bean at night going to bed. In a few nights it will thicken the rheum and prevent its falling upon the wind-pipe'.

None of these are quite so strange as that reported in the *Dorset County Chronicle* of April 3 1834:

The vapours of superstition have not yet been dissipated in the light of education. An elderly dame, last week, ran breathlessly towards a gentleman riding near Taunton on a white horse, eagerly asking him for a remedy for her child who had the whooping cough. The silly creature was referred to a medical gentleman ... but ... insisted that he would not do, no prescription being of the least use unless given by the first person she met on a white horse.

Green Balsam or Oil of Charity

Take red sage, rosemary, lavender, broadleaf balm, camomile, spearmint, bay buds, southernwood, red rose-buds of each four ounces, with rue and wormwood of each two ounces. Gather them on a hot sunshiny day, wipe them with a cloth but don't wash them. Chop them very small and put them in a wide-mouthed bottle and put to them a quart of olive (or the purest) oil you can get and tie it down close and let it stand in the sun for three weeks stirring it once in two or three days. Then put it into a skillet and boil it gently a little and strain out the herbs as hard as you can wring them.

Put into the oil half the quantity of the same herbs fresh gathered as before and let them stand in the sun again three or four days. Set them on the fire which must be very gentle and let it boil very softly till it be a perfect green then strain out the herbs and let the oil stand for a whole night in a pewter basin. Put your basin on a chafing dish of coals. Let the oil boil. If any scum arrives take it off clean and let it stand till it be cold.

Take a little off the top in a glass bottle to keep for special use. Take off the rest and if there be any water in the bottom leave it. This ointment is good to anoint and treat all wounds for it heals at the bottom first and for any inward or outward bruise, sore breast or swelling anoint it twice a day keeping it warm. For an inward bruise take two spoonfuls of it in six of sack making it as hot as you can drink it. To be taken fasting two or three mornings. For a strain or swelling you must mix twice as much brandy as oil. To be made in May.

(Note: a further recipe for 'Green Ointment' uses sixty-eight herbs and plants. 'First your elder buds and poplar buds must be gathered in their season, shred and mixed' with 'ten pounds of good hog's lard' to 'stand till the middle of May. When all the herbs before mentioned must be gathered in the heat of the day, clean wiped, shred and mixed with the lard'. After adding various other ingredients, boiling, clarifying by allowing it to stand for fourteen days it could be used for bruises or sprains).

Hog's lard was also an important ingredient in one particularly adaptable remedy:

A Poultice for Man or Beast
Take a quartern loaf and a quart of skimmed milk. Boil them gently over the fire keeping them continually stirring so by degrees a pint of oatmeal. If it grows too stiff put in more milk then take a quarter of a pound of linseed beat, a pound of white lilyroot stamped small in a marble mortar and a pound of hog's lard. Put them into the poultice and stir them well in for the space of a quarter of an hour over the fire so as to bring them altogether into a soft poultice. Apply one half overnight, the other the next morning and repeat the same as long as you find occasion.

Mr Lathom

An alternative way of treating a 'green wound' was to apply a plaster:

Court or Benjamin Plaster for any Green wound
One ounce of gum benjamin [benzoin] and half an ounce of isinglass. Dissolve them in half a pint of the best brandy over a slow fire, strain it through a piece of muslin and let it stand till it's the consistency of a jelly. Strain a piece of black silk in a frame and brush it over as thin as possible. Let it dry and if it's not perfectly covered and shining brush it over a second time. Send it to a dyer and get him to put it into his hot press and it will shine like glass. Wet the plaster when you apply it.

Swallow Water for Convulsion Fits

Take forty or fifty swallows as soon as they are ready to fly, the more of the swallows the better. Bruise them to a pap in a mortar, feathers and all then add to them two ounces of the best castor in a powder. Put them into a cold still with three pints of the best white wine vinegar. Distil it as any other water. Paste up the head of the still. You may give one or two spoons to a little child sweetened well with the finest sugar, to a bigger child three spoonfuls. This water is good for the passion of the heart, for the fits of the mother, for the falling sickness, for sudden fits, the dead palsy, apoplexy, lethargy or any other impediment proceeding from the head. A spoonful may be given two or three times a day when the fit is off especially three or four days before and after the full of the moon.

A Glister for Fits of any kind particularly Hysteric or Falling Sickness

Take a bladder and wet it in warm water and tie it up as you would for another glister then let somebody that can smoke very well fill the bladder quite out as if it was blowed up. It must be tied very close that no smoke gets out and give it to the patient.

Fits of the Mother

Put a pound of single peony roots well cleaned and sliced very thin into three pints of white wine. Let it infuse twelve twelve hours close stopped in warm embers then strain it out of hand. Take Rusna (?) castor finely powdered a quarter of an ounce, of the best spirit of castor one ounce, the moss of a dead man's skull and of the skull itself each thirty grains finely powdered. Put all these together to the white wine above mentioned and shake the bottle well to incorporate them. Keep it close stopped in a cool place for use.

Dose: one spoonful for a child and a wine glassful for a grown person three mornings together. You may likewise give it in the fit.

N.B. if the person be with child it must not be given lest it cause abortion.

Two other remedies refer to pregnancy:

For Breeding Women

Take one ounce of nutmegs and bake them upon a half quartern loaf. When cold take them out and let the person take half a small nutmeg or a third of a large one going to bed and drink a quarter of a pint of plaster water after it. They are to begin taking them when they are a month or two months gone with child. Take them a month or six weeks or it will be better to continue taking them till they are quick.

The Strengthening Plaster for their Back, Lady Westmorland

Take of choicest mastic four drams, gum elborney half an ounce, of burgundy pitch three drams, benjamin[benzoin] and dragon's blood of each two drams, of the best bolarmonick finely powdered two drams, Venice turpentine a little quantity, one dram of the plaster of red lead made of the oil of quince, half an ounce of beeswax, a dram and a half of Indian balsam, two scruples of the oil of spike. Make all these into a plaster and spread it on Alum leather. Be sure not to let it boil and keep it stirring all the while. They must put on a fresh plaster every three weeks or month and leave it off quite a month before they lie in.

Eighteenth century infant mortality rates were high: of Ambrose and Christiana Awdry's twelve children three were still-born or died in infancy and a fourth, Elizabeth, died aged nine years. The Reverend Walter Post's memorial tablet also records the deaths of his four grand daughters at the ages of five weeks, three and nine months and seven years. It is hardly surprising that the manuscript offers advice:

For a child as soon as born

Give it juice of rue. Some mix soot drops with it to prevent fits. A blister laid on the back has had very good effect on many who could not before raise any child.

Instructions to make the 'soot drops' mentioned above are given much later in the manuscript and are, though poetic, most obscure:

To Make Soot Drops

Take one ounce of soot that is hard, shining and shivering from a country where no coal is burnt, half an ounce of assafedia [asafoetida?] broth beat very fine, half an ounce of Russia castor, a quarter of an ounce of strained galbanum. All these to be infused in a quart of right French Brandy, the bottle to be set in the sun or by the fire to be shook every day.

The new-born child who survived the mixture of rue and soot drops but remained weak might be dosed with a syrup made by boiling 'sweet wort and a handful of sage of virtue' or have her joints rubbed 'morning and evening with the joint oil of a bullock [which your butcher can procure] mixed with rum and well shook together.' For teething a 'necklace of single peony seeds and henbane' was recommended. A mixture of nutmeg, rhubarb and 'Gascoyn's Powder' was one cure suggested for 'children that are griped' the alternative being far worse:

Kill a chicken and take the guts out while it is warm and boil them in water enough to make a glister for the size of the child and give it.

For Convulsion Fits

Take a pigeon alive and pick the feathers off the tail and hold the fundament of the pigeon to the patient's fundament till the pigeon is in convulsions. Repeat it as you see occasion.

However bizarre this remedy it is very close to an item from the *Derby Mercury* of November 30 1797:

On Wednesday last the only child of Stephen Friar Gilham Esq. of Sharfield, Brentwood, Essex, about a month old was seized with convulsions, which were so violent that every moment was expected to be its last. As a last expedient, when everything else failed, one of the servants provided a live pigeon, and plucking the feathers from the breast, applied that part to the pit of the child's stomach, who then lay apparently dead ... the remedy was continued for near three quarters of an hour, at the end of which the child was completely recovered, but the pigeon was so violently convulsed that the servant could with difficulty hold it, and it died a few minutes after, in the utmost agony, having effectually extracted that affection from the child which proved its own destruction ...

An equally alarming cure is one that recommends swallowing mercury:

Loss of Limbs by Cold

Miss Lisle Sister to the Commodore had the use of her limbs taken away by lying in damp sheets and could get no relief by the physicians was cured by taking of quicksilver crude.

Smallpox

Walnuts at pickling time, rue and figs an equal quantity of each bruised, cut and sliced and put into a cold still and drawn off gently to be put into the still in layers. Give to a child a teaspoonful and so increase according to the age to a large spoonful and a half for a grown person. Give it two or three times in the coming out and at the turn the same or if they find them sick sore or if the patient droops. A little sack and saffron is likewise good on some occasions but not while the above is used.

Some will say make milk and water hot and let the patient be set above the knees in it, the body wrapped up in flannel.

Smallpox had first arrived in England in the early sixteenth century, epidemics recurring for the next two centuries until the disease came under a degree of control from vaccination. For those who survived the disease there remained the problem of scarring: in the worst cases it was so disfiguring that some sufferers preferred to remain hidden away for the rest of their lives.

To Preserve the Face from being Pitted with the Smallpox

After the eruption and when the pustules begin to swell and be filled with pus or matter take chalk thoroughly pulverized and mix it with fresh cream so as to make a kind of liquid pomatum that it may the more easily be laid upon the face of the patient for which purpose a feather is to be used. As the pomatum dries the anointing is to be renewed thus the patient will not be tempted to scratch, the coolness of the cream preventing the itching and the chalk with which it is mixed insensibly drying up the matter of the pustules, hinder it from penetrating into the flesh and consequently from pitting. This precaution has benefited all on whom it has been practised.

Bite of a Mad Dog – an Infallible Cure

Take six ounces of rue, clean picked and bruised, four ounces of garlic, picked and bruised, four ounces of Venice treacle, four ounces of scraped tin.

Boil these in two quarts of the best ale in a pan covered close over a gentle fire for the space of one hour then skim the ingredients from the liquor. Give eight or nine spoonfuls of it warm to a man or a woman three mornings fasting and cold to any beast fasting. Eight or nine spoonfuls is sufficient for the strongest. For those younger or of a weaker constitution as you may judge of their strength, ten or twelve spoonfuls for a horse or bullock, three, four or five for a sheep, hog or dog. This must be given within nine days of the bite and never fails either in man or beast. If you can conveniently bind some of the ingredients on the wound. I am able to say in favour of it that I have used it myself and known it applied by others a great many times upon man and beast and always with success.

P.S. I made use of filed pewter and not scraped tin from the Reverend Mr W. Post of Great Cheverill in Wiltshire.

'Four ounces scrapings of pewter' are an ingredient of the cure for the bite of a mad dog recorded in the *Derby Mercury* of 10 May 1792. Added to rue, garlic, Venice treacle, boiled in strong ale and 'kept close corked in a bottle' it was a cure for men, women – and dogs. The cure was obtained 'from Gathorpe church in Lincolnshire, where many persons have been bit by a mad dog. Those who used the medicine recovered; they who did not died mad'.

In case the infallible cure proved fallible the manuscript gives three other cures for the same complaint. Lady Frederick's cure warns 'be sure neither to use the cold bath or bleeding' in contradiction of:

Doctor Mead's Receipt for the Bite of a Mad Dog

Let the patient be blooded nine or ten ounces. Take of the herb called in Latin Lichen *Cinercus terrestis*, in English coloured ground liverwort, cleaned, dried and powdered half an ounce, half an ounce of black pepper powdered two drams. Mix these well together and divide the powder into four doses, one of which must be taken fasting for four mornings successively in half a pint of cow's milk warm. After these four doses are taken the patient must go into the cold bath or a cold spring or river every morning fasting for a month. He must be dipped all over but not stay in (with his head above water) longer than half a minute if the water be very cold. After this he must go in three times a week for a fortnight longer.

The lichen is a very common herb and grows generally in sandy and barren soils all over England. The night to gather it is in October or November.

N.B. Dipping in the sea, after the manner it is usually practised, is of no service at all.   R. Mead

By the mid-eighteenth century infection with the Plague or being bitten by a mad dog was far less likely than infection with tuberculosis or 'consumption'. By 1780 this was one of the major causes of death given in the London Bills of Mortality. The manuscript differentiates between minor coughs which could be cured with mixtures such as linseed, brown sugar candy and orange juice and the more ominous cough 'tending to a consumption'.

Cough

Three golden pippins roasted and put in a teapot with a quarter of an ounce of linseed. Pour half a pint or more of boiling Tilbury water and drink a large glass at bedtime.

The above remedy is clearly preferable to this:

Take a pint of garden snails and put to them a pound of brown sugar candy, prick the snails and tie them in a flannel bag and let them drop in a basin. You may put in a hundred millipedes then sweeten what you drink with it.

Millipedes – 'millipedis' in the manuscript – were, apparently, in the eighteenth century not the insects they are today. The name was an alternative name for wood-lice, Dr Johnson explaining that they were 'so called from their numerous feet'.

Snails were also an important ingredient of the following remedy to cure 'A Consumptive Cough Spitting Blood or a Weak Decaying Constitution':

Take thirty garden snails and bruise them in their shells, as many red earthworms out of a gravelly soil. Take the snails out of their shells and wash both them and the worms. Bruise the snails and cut the worms in pieces. After they are washed put them into three pints of spring water with a spoonful of pearl barley and let it boil till it is wasted to a ninth then strain it and sweeten to your taste with candied eringo root which must be melted in over the fire stirring it all the time.

N.B. Be sure you bruise the snails before they are out of their shells as it is very material. Drink half a pint of it with a small cupful of new milk early in the morning fasting (as warm as milk from the cow) two hours after it. Take the same quantity three hours after dinner.

You must not expect any surprising good effects from it in the first month you drink it. But have patience to go on with it for two months in which time it has recovered many that were given over by several eminent physicians. Miss Bathurst knew a young lady whom it cured after being carried to and from bed for four months.

Two later entries in the book offer variations on the same theme:

Calf's Lung Water

Take a gallon of milk and the lungs of a calf whilst they are warm, a peck of garden snails washed in water then beat them in a mortar till the shells are broken, twelve whites of eggs and four nutmegs pounded. Distil it in a close still and drink a glass three or four times a day sweetened with sugar candy.

The most famous Snail Water

Take a peck of shell garden snails, wash them well in small beer and put them in a hot oven until they are done making a noise then take them out and wipe them clean of the green froth that will be on them. Bruise them, shells and all in a stone mortar. Take a quart of earth worms and scour them with salt. Wash them clean then beat them to pieces and lay them in the bottom of your still. Put angelica, two handfuls of celandine upon them, two quarts of rosemary flowers, boarsfoot, agrimony, red dock root, bark of barberry tree, bettony wood, sorrel of each two handfuls, one handful of rue. Lay the snails upon the herbs then pour on three gallons of the strongest beer if you have it. If not, ale will do. Let it stand all night. Next morning put in three ounces of cloves well beaten, sixpennyworth of beaten saffron (and) on the top of them six ounces of hartshorn shavings. Then set on the Limbeck (the still) and close it with paste. receive the water by pints and when it is all come down mix it unless you keep a pint of it for extraordinary occasions. Take it in the morning two spoonfuls of it in about a glassful of middling ale. Use moderate exercise to warm the blood. It may be still'd in milk for young children and old people adding hartstongue and elecampane.

Ralph Whitlock in *Folklore in Wiltshire* notes that ' ... snail broth used to be regarded as a cure for tuberculosis or consumption as it was then called. The snails, or black slugs would do, were boiled in milk, strained, and served before breakfast'. An alternative and probably more palatable cure was offered in Doctor Mead's 'very good drink for a consumption':

Take sassafras and sarsaparilla of each two handfuls, shavings of hartshorn, liquorice, china root and caraway seeds of each one ounce. Boil all those in eight quarts of water very softly and close covered till it comes to five quarts. Drink as much as you think proper mixed with an equal quantity of new milk boiled. You must drink it warm, and drink no malt liquor nor eat any salt meat whilst you are drinking it. Put it in dry bottles. Ordered by Doctor Mead.

There are numerous other 'waters': Camomile Water for the colic, Aniseed Water 'very good for the wind', Cinnamon Water, Poppy Water and 'Fine Treacle Water' for unspecified ills, Plague Water which needed a gallon of 'good sack or brandy' and 'an Imperial Water' for 'all distempers of the brain, head and stomach'. 'The Great Palsey Water' required fourteen varieties of spices, herbs and flowers infused in brandy for nine months to which were added eighteen pints of lavender flowers, more brandy to 'make ... three gallons' and a further ten ingredients. In comparison the following remedy is simplicity itself:

Hysteric Water
Take juice of poppy, wormwood, pennyroyal, mugwort, hyssop and elderflowers of each an equal quantity. Distil all together and add a little refined sugar in each bottle and keep it for use. This is excellent for all distempers of the matron to be taken by spoonfuls at a time. To two or three ounces nutmeg, one pound of mace, ginger and whole cloves half an ounce each, rhubarb one ounce, spikenard half an ounce, oil of bays two ounces. Let the spices be whole. Put them into seven quarts of the best Rhenish or Canary wine. Digest them in a glass jar close stopped ten days then strain and beat the pulp. Digest them together again three or four days then draw off the water into a limbeck and distil for use. Good against hysteric fits two spoonfuls at a time.

Dropsy
Bathe the part swelled with warm salad oil before the fire every night for a quarter of an hour then swathe it round with Coventry Blue Flannel nine times dipped. Continue it till cured. Take purging salts twice a week during the operation. It may be six weeks before you are sensible of any benefit.
Another
Take leeks and bruise them altogether in a mortar and strain off the juice. Take three tablespoonfuls in half a pint of milk just as

warm as it comes from the cow for nine mornings fasting and then rest for some time and take it again as you find occasion.

N.B. Burdock Tea is another very good thing if the person cannot bear leeks.

The Great Secret to Cure a Dropsy

Take elder leaves, the fairest you can get and lay the smooth side of the leaves next your legs and along the shin bone from the bowing of your knee to the lower part of the instep. The leaves must be laid across the shinbone and to make them stick wet them a little with your spittle on the smooth side. Every morning and evening you must lay on fresh leaves and put on a pair of linen stockings to keep them on for ten days together. And if in the space of half an hour you make water after the leaves are on your legs and the water smell strong of the elder it is a sign you will be perfectly cured in a short time.

The leaves thus applied will cause the making abundance of water and for three days the water will smell of the elder, seldom more, but will still continue the making water during the times the leaves are laid on and the swelling will be quite gone. But if you find you are not perfectly cured in ten days you may use it twenty days and such as have used them so long have been perfectly cured and never had it again. Well approved.

The cures above might have been of some use to Jane Austen's mother. There seems a note of astringency in Jane's letter to her sister, Cassandra, on December 18 1798:

My mother continues hearty, her appetite and nights are very good, but her Bowels are not entirely settled, and she sometimes complains of an Asthma, a Dropsy, Water in her Chest and a Liver disorder.

Some years later she was to comment 'I have not much compassion for colds in the head, without fever or sore throat'. For those whose colds were accompanied by fevers and sore throats the manuscript offers much advice but of the six cures for 'Ague and Fever' only one is 'guaranteed':

Take a quarter of an ounce of Jesuits' Bark, make it into a soft electuary [ointment] with conserve of wormwood and take half of this as soon as the fit is over and the rest twelve hours after it. And after you have taken the electuary take an ounce of (iminstick) steel drops twenty times a day in any liquor you drink till you have taken all the drops. The fever must intermit before it is taken. It was never known to fail. It came from Sir Robert Cotton of Cheshire, a very good and charitable man.

A much pleasanter fever cure is this:

Peach Flower Syrup

Take half a pound of peach flowers and put them into a well-glazed pan. Pour upon them a pint and a half of boiling water. Let it stand a day then strain and press it and add four ounces of fresh flowers more to the liquor and let it stand as before. So do a third time then put to the liquor a pound and a half of double refined sugar and let it simmer to a syrup but not boil.

It gently purges phlegm and choler and represses the force and violence of choleric fevers. Dose two or three ounces.

Jaundice can be cured by taking 'two hundred Hog Lice' which are bruised and 'put to steep in a quart of white wine twenty-four hours'. Fortunately the liquid was strained before taking 'a glass night and morning'. Indigestion and similar problems had numerous cures suggested. A 'sick or disordered stomach' could be cured by taking 'a root of bark, slice it into a tea-pot and pour boiling water on it. Let it stand till it is a strong bitter and drink a cup morning and evening'. Worms were dealt with by drinking 'red wine with salt in it in the morning fasting'. A much more palatable cure is that suggested for colic:

Strawberry Brandy for the Colic or Stone

Put a pint of strawberries into a quart bottle. Fill it up with brandy and cork it down. Let it stand a month then bottle it off. To be taken either mixed with water or without.

Less pleasant was a mixture of 'four powders', rhubarb, caraway, cream of tartar and licorice, which when mixed together were to be kept and ' ... whenever you find the colic a-coming take as much as will lay on two shillings in any liquor you like or at any time of the day, even as soon as you have dined'.

Dr Lower's Tincture for the Colic

Take of guiacum chips, elecampane roots, licorice sliced, coriander seeds prepared and bruised, senna of Alexandria of each two ounces, half a pound of raisins of the sun stoned. Infuse these in three quarts of small aniseed water ten or twelve days in a stone jug close stopped. Shake or stir them every day then pour off the clear fluid and put it into bottles for use. You may add one ounce of sweet fennel seeds bruised.

Note: to prepare the coriander seeds you must steep them in white wine vinegar twelve hours then dry them in the sun or by the fire. Give three spoonfuls of this tincture in a fit of the colic. If that does not operate or ease the pain you may repeat the same dose three or four hours after or a less quantity according to the age and strength of the patient, so continuing till it has passed downwards.

A comprehensive remedy is for 'obstructions and divers infirmities learned of a Jesuit who confessed he got four or five hundred a year by it'.

Take a pound and a half of unslaked lime. Let it stand eight hours in a gallon of spring water then take it gently off with a thin skimming dish. Put into it liquorice, aniseeds, sassafras sliced of each a quarter of a pound, one pound of blue currants, beaten mace a quarter of an ounce. Let them be infused in the aforesaid water one night then pour the liquor from the ingredients and keep it for use. Drink half a pint with a spoonful of syrup of violets a little warm three times a day viz. an hour before breakfast, dinner and supper and a little after it walk gently about. Good against all manner of obstructions and all kind of ulcers inward or outward. It may likewise be used by way of injection.

Gout

Take polypody of the oak, hermedaetlys, chinaroot and sarsaparilla of each an ounce, guiacum six ounces. Infuse these in nine pints of water and three of white wine sliced or bruised in a close covered pot or pipkin twenty four hours over a moderate fire. After this has stood infusing let it boil gently to the consumption of a fourth part then strain off the liquor for use. The same ingredients will serve again to make two decoctions more with six pints of water and two of wine boiling and straining them as before. Drink for three days as much as you reasonably can for the more you drink (so as not to offend the stomach) the sooner will the cure be effected. While you are drinking this decoction abstain from broths, salads, sauces, fruit, milk or anything made. You may eat of any well-roasted meat that is easy of digestion but not salted. On every third or fourth day take a gentle purge for fear you break out in boils. Afterwards while you are drinking this decoction forbear all other liquors. If this method be followed there is no gout, rheumatism or defluxion whatever but will yield to it and was scarce ever known to fail of a cure. If you find this has any effect on you and once taking it does not make a perfect cure take it a second time and you'll hardly fail of your wishes. It is a great purifier of the blood. It is only alterative and works only by the urine unless you take the physic prescribed which must by no means be neglected for the reasons before ascribed. Be sure and follow these directions exactly. If you fail of a cure it will be owing to your neglect. It cured the Reverend Doctor Green of Coleson in Wiltshire when his nerves were contracted.

Of the various cures for Rheumatism the simplest is a 'tea' of dried elder flowers. The patient is advised to 'drink half a pint in a morning and walk after it. This has done great cures'. Others came with personal recommendations:

For the Rheumatism

Eight ounces of guiacum chips, three ounces of sassafras, one ounce of sarsaparilla, one ounce of chinaroot, two ounces of licorice root sliced, two ounces of juniper berries, one ounce of coriander seeds bruised, eight ounces of raisins of the sun cut, eight ounces of antimony coarsely powdered and tied up in a bag. Boil these ingredients in six quarts of spring water close covered up till it comes to about a gallon then strain it off and put one quart of good old rum or the very best of geneva [gin] to it and a pound of loaf sugar. Drink half a pint as hot as a dish of tea morning, noon and night for two months together twice in the year when you may be got well of the fit, the best of which are March and April then rest till October and November. Given by Sir Edward Hulse to Mr Smith in the Borough, Brazier, Southwark who was perfectly cured by it and by him to several others with the like success.

Another cure for rheumatism was said to have 'cured Mrs Winter's cook when she was on the rack every night' and the following versatile remedy was obtained from a member of the Delmé family:

To make a Pomade Divine

Take a pound and a half of beef marrow clean from bones and strings. Put it into an earthen vessel filled with spring water. Shift it night and morning for ten days then steep it in a pint of rose water for twenty-four hours. Drain it after that quite dry in a linen cloth. The dry resin of the tree called the gum of the benjamin tree – one dram of benzoin, one dram of cypress powder, the odoriferous sort, one dram of ornence [?] of Florence, one ounce of storax, half an ounce of cinnamon, two drams of cloves, two drams of nutmegs all finely powdered and mixed with the marrow. Put all these ingredients in a pewter pot shaped like an ice pot with close cover and two handles of three pints size, well made and extremely well joined. Tie the lid fast down by the handles and sew a piece of cloth very tight round the cover. Paste it round with a paste made of the white of an egg and flour. Bind it on with another piece of cloth that nothing may evaporate within.

Put the pot in a copper full of water supported by two sticks through the handles which are to rest on the top of the copper. There must be water enough in the copper that it may not touch anything and it must boil three hours without losing a moment. In order to do that you must have boiling water always ready to supply your copper as the other wastes by boiling, so that it may be always the same fullness. Strain it through a linen cloth and put it into small pots for use. Cover it not till it's cold. Never touch it with anything but silver or your finger in using it.

N.B. 'Tis good for bruises, piles or any other inflammations. Mrs Delmé cured a person going to be cut for a fistula by it, and a man who was near starved by a sore mouth of five or six months standing eat holes by canker or cancer [was cured] by melting some into a silver spoon and anointing the tongue and mouth with a feather.

Two cures for 'stomatick gout' which could also be used for rheumatism are attributed to Dr Cheney. His 'Burgundy' combines various herbs with orange peel, cardamom seeds and cochineal. The mixture is then infused in 'five half pints of mountain' and strained off after standing forty-eight hours by the fire. The second cure is similar:

Dr Cheney's Bishop
Two ounces of Rhubarb sliced, one ounce of Jesuit bark, two seville oranges roasted and sliced, of juniper berries, cardamoms and cochineal each a dram. Infuse it in a quart of mountain for a week then strain it off. You may put a quart of brandy or mountain on the same ingredients after the first is off. To be taken four spoonfuls twice a day. Good as the former in the gout.

Headache
Mace, nutmegs, pepper, allspice, cinnamon, cloves of each an equal quantity beat very fine and put into a muslin bag and laid on top of the head.

Another

Take some rue and bruise it and apply it to the head. A very good thing and has been known to cure madness.

Six pages of the manuscript are occupied by a variety of 'syrups' and 'conserves' of herbs and flowers. 'Syrup of Vinegar' adds vinegar, hyssop and rosemary to ' ... licorice sliced in a silver tankard ... this syrup is very opening and cuts the phlegm and is therefore very good for a cold'. 'Syrup of Roses Solative' uses damask roses to make a syrup which ' ... purges choler gently and pleasantly. Being given in clarified whey three ounces at a time it cools and loosens the belly and expels phlegm'. Some syrups were remarkably versatile: Syrup of Marshmallow Compound could ' ... provoke urine, cleanse the passages, break and expel gravel in both the reins [bowels] and bladder, give ease to intolerable pains in these parts ... prevalent against the colic and heals a dysentery'. A Syrup of Jerusalem Oak Compound is for a variety of problems with the lungs ... I keep it for use. It is good for coughs, colds, asthmas, ulcers of the lungs, spitting of blood, pains of the side ... and consumptions'.

The manuscript's most original remedy is a rhyming cure 'for an Asthma'

Marcus old friend, accept of me
The following rules, without a fee
An asthma is your case, I think
So you must neither eat nor drink
(I mean) of meats, preserved in salt
Nor any liquors made of malt.
From seasoned sauce avert your eyes,
From hams, and tongues, and pigeon pies.
If venison pasty's set before ye
Each bit you eat memento mori
Your supper, nothing if you please,
But, above all, no toasted cheese.
'tis likely, you will now observe
What I prescribe will make you starve.
No; I allow you at a meal
A neck, a loin or leg of veal.
Young turkeys I allow you four,
Partridge, pullets, half a score,
Of house lamb boiled eat quarters two,
The Devil's in it if that won't do.
Now as to liquor, why indeed
Might I advise, it should be mead.
Glasses of wine, to extinguish drought,
Drink two with water, three without.
Let constant exercise be tried
And sometimes walk and sometimes ride.
Health's oftener found on Highgate Hill
Than in the Apothecary's pill.
Be not in haste, or think to do
Your business with a Purge or two.
Some if they are not well at once
Proclaim their doctor for a dunce.
Restless from quack to quack they range
When 'tis themselves they ought to change.
Nature hates violence and force,
By method led and gentle course.
Rules and restraints you must endure
Ills brought by time 'tis time must cure.

The Use of vegetables try
And prize Pomona in a pie.
Young Bacchus' rites you must avoid
And leave fair Venus unenjoyed.
Whate'er you take, put something good in
And worship Ceres in a pudding.
For breakfast it is my advice
Eat gruel, sago, barley, rice.
Take burdock roots and by my troth
I'd mingle daisies in my broth
Thus you with ease may draw your breath
Deluding, what you dread not, Death
Laugh with your friends, be gay and thrive,
Enrish'd by those whom you survive.

115

Glossary

Agrimony: Wild agrimony is a variety of potentilla. Culpeper describes Agrimonia Eupatoria as a herb which 'openeth and cleanseth the liver, helpeth the jaundice, and is very beneficial to the bowels, healing all inward wounds, bruises, hurts and other distempers'.

Allspice: *Pimenta officinalis* – also known as Jamaica pepper. Used in marinades for meat or fish, as an ingredient of pot pourri and in some sweet dishes.

Alum: A whitish transparent mineral salt with astringent qualities. Used in the nineteenth century to adulterate bread and flour.

Angelica: *Herba angelica* – 'the angelic plant'. Used in cookery and medicine. A piece of angelica root held in the mouth was believed to ward off 'pestilential aires' and guard against the Plague. Candied angelica stalks are first recorded in 1653.

Antimony: A brittle, metallic substance. Blue-white in colour, crystalline in texture, used in alchemy, pharmacy and chemistry.

Asafoetida: Resinous gum obtained from the plant *Narthex Asafoetida*. Used in cookery and also in medicine as an anti-spasmodic.

Barberries: Berries of the berberis shrub.

Basil: Apart from its use in cookery basil was believed to 'cure the infirmities of the heart' and to be a cure for melancholy.

Bay leaves: *Laurus nobilis* – the leaves of the bay tree have been used in cookery since ancient times. Culpeper believed that' ... neither witch nor devil, thunder nor lightning, will hurt a man where a bay tree is'.

Bay salt: First produced in France and later in Spain and Portugal by evaporating sea water. This produced a dark, coarse-grained salt which was cheaper than refined salt and particularly effective as a preserving salt for meat and fish. By the sixteenth century the term also came to mean a mixture of coarse salt and herbs.

Benjamin: Gum benjamin or gum benzoin – an aromatic tree resin used in cosmetics for its astringent qualities and also as incense.

Bettony Wood: *Betonica officinalis* or wood betony used medicinally since Roman times and, according to Culpeper, it could cure ' old and filthy ulcers; yea though they be fistulous and hollow ... being applied with a little hog's lard it helpeth a plague or sore and other biles or pushes'.

Bolarmonick: *Johnson's Dictionary* of 1755 gives the definition of 'Bole' as 'a kind of earth' and 'bole Armeniack' as a type of earth with astringent qualities originating in Armenia.

Bullace: A type of small damson with a very sharp taste used to add colour. Also sold as a dried fruit.

Caraway: Used in cookery and medicine since the sixteenth century. Sugar-coated caraway seeds, 'caraway comfits' were also used as an aid to digestion and as breath-sweeteners.

Cardamom: A pale green pod containing a number of highly aromatic small, black seeds cardamom is an important ingredient in Middle Eastern cookery. With cinnamon, ginger, cloves, mace, nutmeg and other expensive imports cardamom was one of the long list of spices used to season sweet and savoury dishes in the Middle Ages.

Carmine: An intense red colouring matter for food and cosmetics obtained from cochineal.

Cayenne Pepper: Powdered form of capsicum used to add intense flavour to spiced dishes.

The manuscript spelling is *cian* – the modern spelling was first recorded in 1756.

Chocolate: First imported and sold in England in the mid-seventeenth century. Chocolate houses, like coffee houses, became fashionable meeting places. Although originally known as a drink recipes using chocolate can be found in seventeenth century recipe books. The manuscript has a recipe for chocolate almonds which were first imported to England from France in the 1670s.

Chinaroot: The thick fleshy root-stock of the plant *Smilax china*, first imported to England at the end of the sixteenth century. Used as a flavouring for ale.

Cinnamon: Aromatic spice derived from dried tree-bark.

Citron: Related to, but distinct from, the lemon. A sharp-tasting oval citrus fruit from the tree Citrus Medica. The peel was candied as a sweetmeat or used in cakes and puddings.

Cloves: Cloves are the dried buds of the evergreen tree *eugenia carophyllus*. Their name comes from the Latin word for a nail, *clavus*.

Cochineal: Intensely red food colouring obtained from a type of Mexican beetle.

Codlin[g]s: Variety of apple with long, tapered shape.

Collops: Slices of fish or meat, particularly, from the fourteenth century onwards, bacon. The word is of Scandinavian origin coming from the Swedish word for coal, kol and leap, huppa. So kolhuppadher would be meat roasted on coals which, presumably, might leap in the pan!

Comfits: Sugar-coated seeds, usually caraway or coriander. Sometimes used as remedies for indigestion.

Cooley: Eighteenth-century spelling of coulis or puree.

Copperas: Sulphate of iron, green vitriol.

Coriander: Mediterranean in origin, coriander seeds have been found in Bronze Age excavations in Southern England.

Cypress Powder: Juniper berries come from a shrub of the cypress family. The term may mean powdered juniper berries. Alternatively Culpeper lists the nuts of the *Cupressus* or Cypress tree as being a cure for, amongst other afflictions, 'fluxes of all kinds ... they prevent the bleeding of the gums and fasten loose teeth'.

Dragon's Blood: Possibly an extract of the plant *Dracontium*, commonly known as Dragon.

Elder Vinegar: *Sambucus nigra* provided elder flowers and berries for a variety of medicinal and culinary purposes. Apart from elderberry wine and vinegar the elderflowers can be used to give a muscat flavour to gooseberries. Cosmetic uses included lotions to prevent wrinkles and to alleviate sunburn.

Electuary: An ointment or medicine in which a powder is mixed with oils, honey or syrups.

Eringo Root: *Eryngium maritimum* or sea holly. Used in a variety of remedies, the roots were sometimes candied. Grown today for its decorative blue thistle-like flowers.

Five Leaf Grass: The plant *potentilla reptans* or cinquefoil.

Flummery: First recorded in 1618 to mean a dish thickened with wheat meal or oatmeal. From the middle of the eighteenth century it also came to mean nonsense or foolishness.

Forcemeat: A term first used in 1688 to describe a savoury stuffing of finely chopped meat combined with herbs and breadcrumbs.

119

Galbanum: A species of gum resin from the Persian plant Ferula.

Galingale: An aromatic plant root popular as a spice and much used in medieval cookery. In the sixteenth century the name 'English galingale' was given to the aromatic root of the plant *Cyperus longus*.

Gallipot: A small, glazed earthen pot of the type used by apothecaries as a container for ointments. John Aubrey described the inhabitants of North Wiltshire as 'plump and feggy' with 'gallipot eyes'.

Galls: Oak-galls are a growth found on the oak tree, used in the production of ink, dyes and tannin.

Gamboge: A substance derived from gum resin. Now used as a pigment because of its intense yellow colour it is also described as a 'drastic purgative'.

Geneva: Gin – from the Dutch *genever*, a spirit flavoured with juniper berries. Until 1736 spirits were taxed at a few pence a gallon. Hogarth's engravings show the effects of cheap spirits:

Drunk for a penny
Dead drunk for twopence

By the mid-eighteenth century there was an estimated annual production of nine million gallons of gin but this fell rapidly when excise duties were increased in an attempt to curb the excesses of 'gin mania'.

Glister: An alternative spelling of clyster, an injection or enema.

Ground Ivy: The berries of ivy, *Hedera helix*, were reputed to be a cure for the Plague.

Ground Liverwort: Culpeper says that not only is liverwort, hepatica, 'a singular good herb for all diseases of the liver' but that also it 'is recommended for the bites of mad dogs'.

Guiacum Chips: The guaiacum tree is a native of the West Indies. The wood of the tree, *lignum vitae*, and the resin were imported for use in medicines from the sixteenth century onwards.

Gum Arabic: Stiffening agent used in sweets such as Turkish Delight

Gum Dragon: Gum tragacanth, used as a stiffening agent in sweets, jellies, marzipan and other sweets.

Hartshorn: Shavings from the horns of the hart, used for their ammonia content. Sometimes used as an ingredient of flummery. Salt of hartshorn is carbonate of ammonia or smelling salts.

Hasty Pudding: The term was first used in 1599 to denote a pudding that could be made quickly. Usually a boiled pudding in which milk was thickened with flour or oatmeal.

Henbane: The plant *Hyoscyamus niger* from which could be extracted a narcotic and potentially poisonous substance.

Hyssop: Several species of which the most common is Hyssopus officinalis. A pungent herb, Mediterranean in origin , with a wide variety of medicinal and culinary uses.

Indian Balsam: Indian balm or balsam is the purple Trillium, *Trillium pendulum*.

Isinglass: A whitish, semi-transparent form of gelatine, obtained from freshwater fish. Used to clarify beer and as a setting agent.

Jagging Iron: An implement which produced an ornamentally indented edge.

Jesuits' Bark: The bark of Cinchona from which quinine is obtained.

Laudanum: The term, which is now used for tincture of opium, was previously used for any preparation in which opium was the major ingredient.

Laurel: Although there are numerous species of laurel the most likely one is *Laurus nobilis*, which is the bay tree.

Linseed: The seed of the flax plant, source of linseed oil and also used medicinally.

Logwood: The dye or drug extracted from the American tree *Haemotoxylon campechianum*.

Mace: Spice from the reddish outer covering of the nutmeg.

Madeira Wine: The description Madeira wine was first applied to the sweet white wine produced in the island towards the end of the sixteenth century. It was first imported to England in the seventeenth century.

Manchet: The finest kind of white bread.

Marjoram: The cultivated form of the wild herb oregano.

Marrow: The marrow from beef marrow bones was commonly used to enrich sweet dishes.

Mastic: An acid resin or gum, varieties obtained from different species of tree were used in making varnish and also as a flavouring.

Mugwort: *Artemisia Vulgaris* or Common Mugwort was recommended by Culpeper as 'excellent in female disorders' and 'the herb itself, being fresh ... is a special remedy upon the over-much taking of opium'.

Muscadine Wine: Wine made from the Muscatel grape.

Mustard Seeds: Both black and white mustard seeds have been used as a condiment since the fourth century.

Naples Biscuits: A type of sweet crisp biscuit, an important ingredient in a number of sweet dishes. The crumbs could also be used as a thickening agent.

Nonpareil: A term used to describe firstly a size of type, later a kind of comfit and, from 1731, a type of apple.

Nutmeg: Used not only as a spice but also medicinally, nutmeg was used as a preventative against the Plague.

Orange-flower water: An aqueous solution of orange flowers used in cosmetics and also as a flavouring.

Pennyroyal : A species of mint with strong peppermint odour.

Peony Roots: Peony roots infused in sack were thought to cure epilepsy.

Peruvian Bark: The bark of the Cinchona tree.

Polypody of the Oak: *Polypody vulgare*, a type of fern, also known as Polypody of the Wall.

Pomatum: A scented ointment or pomade, the name derived from the Latin *pomum*, apple.

Pomegranate: The fruit was first brought to Europe from Africa by the Moors and was incorporated into the coat of arms of the royal family of Aragon. Mary Tudor included it in her own coat of arms in memory of her mother, Catherine of Aragon.

Posset: A drink, sometimes medicinal, in which milk was heated and then curdled with the addition of wine or ale.

Quicksilver: Mercury.

Quinces: Hard, acid, yellowish pear-shaped fruit used in preserves.

Ragout: The use of the term, borrowed from the French, to describe a dish of stewed meat, is first recorded in 1664.

Red Lead: Red lead ore or crocoite.

Rosemary: An aromatic herb extremely popular by the sixteenth century and used in many dishes, it also had various medicinal and cosmetic uses. Sir Thomas More said 'I lette it run all over my garden walls'.

Rosewater: Water distilled from roses or scented with essence of roses. Used as a perfume but also as a flavouring in creams and syllabubs.

Rue: A perennial evergreen shrub with bitter, strongly-scented leaves.

Sack: A dry amber wine from Spain first imported to England during the reign of Henry VIII and believed to aid digestion.

Saffron: An aromatic yellow spice obtained from the stamens of the Crocus *sativus*. At one time grown in England at Saffron Walden but now imported. The most expensive spice.

Sage: *Salvia*, the healing plant.

Salamander: A metal implement heated in an open fire and then held close to the surface of food to produce a crisp, brown finish.

Salop: A drink or jelly made from the dried tubers of orchidaceous plants.

Saltpetre: A crystalline substance, potassium nitrate, the main ingredient of gun-powder.

Sal Volatile: Ammonium carbonate, used to restore consciousness after fainting.

Sarsaparilla: The roots of the smilax plant.

Sassafras: A North American tree, an infusion of the dried bark was first used for medicinal purposes in the sixteenth century.

Saunders: A red colouring used in food, especially gingerbread.

Senna: The dried leaves of the Cassia shrub, used as a purgative and emetic.

Smalt: A blue dye, oxide of cobalt.

Southernwood: A deciduous shrub, *Artemisia abrotanum*, originating in southern Europe and cultivated for medicinal purposes.

Spermaceti: A fatty substance found in the head of the sperm-whale.

Spikenard: An aromatic oil obtained from plants found in Northern India.

Stone Blue: A compound of indigo dye and starch used in laundering linen.

Storax: A fragrant resin obtained from the tree *styrax officinalis*.

Suckets: Sweets made from candied citron peels.

Tamarind: The fruit of the tree *Tamarindus indica*.

Tansy: A strongly aromatic herb – the term later came to mean a dish flavoured with tansy. By the eighteenth century this was most likely to be a sweet dish of some kind.

Treacle: Originally used medicinally most treacle used in England was imported, first from Venice and later from Genoa and Flanders By the late seventeenth century refineries had been set up in London.

Truffles: An edible fungus which develops underground.

Wormwood: A variety of Artemisia, known for its bitter taste. According to Culpeper Roman Wormwood *Artemisia pontica* was used to make a flavoured wine '...the Germans drink of it so often, that they are able to eat for hours together, without sickness or indigestion.'

Bibliography

A Cornish Anthology, A.L. Rowse (Macmillan 1968)

A History of Make-up, Maggie Angeloglou (Studio Vista 1970)

A History of the Cost of Living, John Burnett (Penguin Books 1969)

A Jane Austen Household Book, Peggy Hickman (David and Charles 1977)

And the Bride Wore ... The Story of the White Wedding, Ann Monsarrat (Gentry Books 1973)

Bath and the Eighteenth Century Novel, Mary K. Hill (Bath University Press 1989)

British Domestic Design Through the Ages, Keogh (Arthur Barker Ltd 1970)

Cottage Economy, William Cobbett (O.U.P. 1979)

Culpeper's Complete Herbal, Nicholas Culpeper (Foulsham)

Dialect in Wiltshire, Malcolm Jones and Patrick Dillon (Wiltshire County Council Museum and Library Service 1987)

Elinor Fettiplace's Receipt Book, Elizabethan Country House Cooking, Hilary Spurling (Viking Salamander 1986)

Fireside Cooks and Black Kettle Recipes, Doris E. Farrington (Bobbs-Merrill, USA 1976)

Folklore and Odysseys of Food and Medicinal Plants, E. and J. Lehner (Harrar, Straus, Giroux, USA 1962)

Food and Drink in Britain, C. Anne Wilson (Constable 1973)

Food in England, Dorothy Hartley (Macdonald and Co. 1954)

Georgian Meals and Menus, Maggie Black (Kingsmead Press, 1977)

Herbs for All Seasons, Rosemary Hemphill (Angus and Robertson 1972)

Herbs in Nutrition, Maria Geuter (Bio-dynamic Agricultural Association 1962)

Illustrated English Social History, Volume Three, G.M. Trevelyan (Longmans, Green 1949-52)

Jane Grigson's Fruit Book, Jane Grigson (Michael Joseph 1982)

Jane Grigson's Vegetable Book, Jane Grigson (Michael Joseph 1978)

London Life in the Eighteenth Century, M. Dorothy George (Kegan, Paul, Trench, Trubner and Co. Ltd. 1925)

Mrs Groundes-Peace's Old Cookery Notebook, Zara Groundes-Peace (Rainbird Reference Books/The Cookery Book Club 1971)

News from the Countryside 1750-1850, Clifford Morsley (Harrap 1979)

Northanger Abbey, Jane Austen (First edition 1818)

Old Cook Books, Eric Quayle (Studio Vista 1978)
Origins of Rhymes, Stories and Sayings, Jean Harrowven (Kaye
    and Ward 1977)
Pepys at Table, Seventeenth Century Recipes for the Modern Cook,
Christopher Driver and Michelle Berriedale-Johnson (Bell
    and Hyman 1984)
Plenty and Want, John Burnett (Thomas Nelson 1966)
Recipes from an Old Farmhouse, Alison Uttley (Faber and Faber
    1966)
Seend: A Wiltshire Village Past and Present, Edward Bradby (Alan
    Sutton Publishing 1981)
Seven Centuries of English Cooking, Maxine McKendry (Weidenfeld
    and Nicolson 1973)
Shops and Shopping 1800-1914, Alison Adburgham (George Allen
    and Unwin 1964)
Spices, Salt and Aromatics in the English Kitchen, Elizabeth David
    (Penguin Books 1970)
The Art of Eating, M.F.K. Fisher (Faber 1963)
The Best of Eliza Acton, edited by Elizabeth Ray (Longmans, Green
    and Company 1968)
The Chocolate Book, Helge Rubinstein (Macdonald and Company
    1981)
*The Compleat Book or the Secrets of a Seventeenth Century
    Housewife by Rebecca Price*, introduced by Madeleine
    Masson (Routledge and Kegan Paul 1974)
The Cookery of England, Elisabeth Ayrton (Andre Deutsch 1974)
The Diary of a Georgian Shopkeeper, Thomas Turner (Oxford
    University Press 1979)
The Englishman's Flora, Geoffrey Grigson (Hart Davis, MacGibbon)
The Folklore of Wiltshire, Ralph Whitlock (Batsford 1976)
The Gardener's and Planter's Calendar, Sir Richard Weston
    (T. Carnan 1778)
The Gardener's Folklore, Margaret Baker (David and Charles 1977)
The Parkers at Saltram 1769-89, Ronald Fletcher
    (BBC Publications 1976)
The Paston Letters, Ed. James Gairdner (Alan Sutton 1986)
The Shocking History of Advertising, E.S. Turner (Michael Joseph
    1952)
Women's Magazines 1693-1968, Cynthia L.White (Michael Joseph
    1970)

COUNTRY BOOKSHELF

from Ex Libris Press presents the following books:

GRAN'S OLD-FASHIONED REMEDIES, WRINKLES AND RECIPES by Jean Penny

Remedies for common ailments; wrinkles, or tips, to save time and effort about the house; recipes using inexpensive ingredients to create mouth-watering dishes: all are included within these pages.
96 pages; Numerous engravings; Price £3.50

GRAN'S OLD-FASHIONED GARDENING GEMS
by Jean Penny

Everyone loves a garden in bloom but few of us are prepared to put in the work needed to create one, and fewer still have the necessary know-how. Packed full of tips and details aimed at the reluctant gardener for whom the 'garden in bloom' is more often 'that blooming garden.'
96 pages; Numerous engravings; Price £3.50

THE ROMANY WAY by Irene Soper

At times anecdotal, at times factual, but always sympathetic and informative, this book is a joyous but gentle celebration of a unique people.
112 pages; Fully illustrated ; Price £4.95

LETTERS FROM THE ENGLISH COUNTRYSIDE
by Ralph Whitlock

Topics included here are firmly rooted in the traditional life of the countryside. There is a good deal of interest to the naturalist, with discussions on various species, from butterflies to badgers. Much attention is also given to agricultural techniques and country customs. A nostalgic but wry view of the past is balanced by an often humorous commentary on the present.
160 pages; Numerous pen & ink drawings; Price £4.95

MARCH WINDS & APRIL SHOWERS
by Ralph Whitlock

'March Winds and April Showers' is one of the better known of scores of traditional sayings relating to the matter of weather forecasting which the author has collected together in this little book.
80 pages; Illustrated with Bewick engravings; Price £3.50

LAND GIRL by Anne Hall
Her story of six years in the Women's Land Army, 1940-46
One woman's recollection of six years dedicated to the Women's Land Army. The many photographs and the author's text combine to produce an honest, evocative and personal portrayal of a unique chapter in our social history.
144 pages; Illustrated throughout; Price £4.95

LUMBER JILL by Mavis Williams
Her story of four years in the Women's Timber Corps, 1942-45
A personal account of a time when women used primitive methods to cut down trees to make pit-props for the coal mines and fuel to produce charcoal.
96 pages; Illustrated; Price £3.95

BELT & BUCKLE by Toby Dyer
An hilarious tale of a west country boyhood
An old-fashioned fruit cake of a book – rich, well-spiced and beautifully presented. It should be forbidden reading in doctor's waiting rooms – to do so would be to risk being ejected for disturbing the other patients; that is, if you don't first die of laughing.
160 pages; line drawings; Price £4.95

WINIFRED by Sylvia Marlow
Her childhood and early working life
Winifred Spencer was born in 1899, the daughter of a cowman and his wife and one of thirteen children. Unsentimental and honest, this is Winifred's story of her struggle to survive.
128 pages; Illustrated throughout; Price £4.50

MAISIE & ME by Stella Ashton
A Country Childhood in the 1920s
The sights, sounds and smells of the countryside come alive in Stella Ashton's recollections of her childhood. Words and pictures combine to produce a loving portrait of a world past, but not forgotten.
80 pages; pen & ink drawings; Price £3.95

These books may be obtained through your local bookshop or direct from the publisher, post-free, at
1 The Shambles, Bradford on Avon, Wiltshire, BA15 1JS.

In addition to the above books, Ex Libris Press also publishes books on the West Country and the Channel Islands. Please ask for our free illustrated list.